ART AT HOME

ART AT
HOME

AN ACCESSIBLE GUIDE TO
COLLECTING & CURATING
ART IN YOUR HOME

RACHEL LOOS

with photography by
CHRIS TUBBS

RYLAND PETERS & SMALL
LONDON • NEW YORK

For photography credits and
copyright information, see page 172.

Published in 2023 by Ryland Peters & Small
20–21 Jockey's Fields
London WC1R 4BW
and
341 East 116th Street
New York, NY 10029

www.rylandpeters.com

10 9 8 7 6 5 4 3 2 1

ISBN 978-1-78879-562-3

A CIP record for this book is available
from the British Library.

Library of Congress CIP data
has been applied for.

Printed and bound in China

Senior designer Toni Kay
Editor Sophie Devlin
Location research Jess Walton
Production manager Gordana Simakovic
Senior commissioning editor Annabel Morgan
Creative director Leslie Harrington

MIX
Paper from
responsible sources
FSC
www.fsc.org   FSC® C106563

CONTENTS

BRING YOUR WALLS TO LIFE

Art was once considered to be the preserve of people with bulging wallets and an art consultant on speed dial, but not any more. Today, thanks to the digital world, the art market has become far more democratic and, dare I say it, fun. Instead of achingly cool bricks-and-mortar art galleries, nowadays you will find a friendlier breed of gallery owner and an abundance of online platforms selling art at affordable prices. Moreover, increasing numbers of artists now post their work directly on social media and are happy to chat to prospective buyers.

All of this means that it has never been easier to decorate your home with art. This is fabulous news, because art is a brilliant way of creating a home that looks and feels amazing. Research has shown that we feel happiest in homes that reflect our personality and art allows you to achieve exactly that. Whether it be a colourful painting that makes your heart sing, a photograph that reminds you of a much-loved holiday or a vintage piece that you fell in love with, art is the decorative finishing touch that will give your home warmth and atmosphere.

Despite all the recent changes, though, many of us still find it daunting to buy art and decide how and where to display it at home. If you've never bought art before or would like to learn more about how to go about it, what do you need to know? This book aims to answer your questions and give you the confidence to start bringing art into your space. I've spoken to a range of experts and pulled together their advice to create a book that covers all the essentials, from the difference between original works and limited-edition prints to the main artistic genres you might encounter. You will also find tips on starting a collection and choosing art for every room in your home, as well as chapters on framing and hanging. I hope you will find this book useful and treat it as your go-to guide for all things art in the home. Happy collecting!

OPPOSITE A large contemporary abstract painting by Thaiwijit Puangkasemsomboon fits in perfectly with the textural modern decor of this room.

PAGES 8–9 Pressed seaweed artworks from Molesworth & Bird hang on a rough, mottled wall that resembles lichen on stone (left). In a period home, traditional panelling frames an old black-and-white map and two portraits in complementary tones (right).

ET IN ARCADIA EGO

WHAT IS ART?

So, what exactly is art? It comes in many forms, including literature and music, but visual art can be defined as a piece of creative work by an artist in which they interpret and convey their feelings about an aspect of the world around them.

The artist hopes that when viewing the artwork, you will not only find it arresting to look at, but that its theme speaks to you in some way and affects you on an emotional level; perhaps the artwork brings back memories of a wonderful summer holiday, or it connects with an emotion about love or loss. In this book, we will primarily be looking at the most popular forms of art found in the home: paintings, prints and photography.

Let's start with a bit of technical information. The material used to create an artwork on paper or canvas is called a medium. The most commonly used is paint. Oil paints are a mix of coloured pigments with an oil such as linseed. Acrylics, watercolours and gouache are all water-based – acrylics are fast-drying with an opaque finish, whereas watercolours allow the white of the paper to show through. Gouache has a white pigment added to make it opaque, but is less durable than acrylic. Then there are pastels (powdered pigments held together by a binding agent and moulded into sticks), charcoal (wood, traditionally willow, that is heated without oxygen to create black crumbly sticks), inks and pencils (often called graphite). There are also specialist mediums such as resin, which has a bright and shiny finish.

Some artists like to play with texture to create three-dimensional hung artworks. These can be made using collage, the process of gluing pieces of paper, canvas, fabric or other materials to create a textured look and feel. Clay and other mediums more often used in sculpture can also be applied to make a three-dimensional artwork.

Photography, once associated with family portraits or professional newspaper and magazine images, is now popular as choice for art in the home. Photographs can be combined with other, more traditional mediums to create eye-catching displays.

PAGES 10-11 On a long storage unit, a mix of modern and vintage art propped against the wall forms a chic backdrop to a collection of decorative objects.

OPPOSITE This room is a successful blend of different styles and eras, including a painting by Nyilyari Tjapangati, thanks to a neutral colour palette that holds it all together.

ART JARGON

There is a huge variety of terms within the art world – these are ones you're most likely to come across

C-print: *a photographic print made from a colour negative*

Composition: *the arrangement of elements within an artwork*

Diptych: *a set of two painted or carved panels*

Edition: *the total number of prints made from an original design*

Genre: *types of painting such as portrait and still life*

Gestural: *painting with a brush in free, sweeping strokes*

Medium: *the material an artwork is made with – this word can also be used to describe a type of art, such as painting*

Mixed media: *made with more than one material*

Monochrome: *in only one colour*

Montage: *a single artwork made with numerous linked images*

Motif: *a re-occuring pattern*

Oeuvre: *an artist's body of work*

Painterly: *a style of painting in which you can see visible brushstrokes*

Photomontage: *a collage made from photographs*

Salon-style hang: *a gallery wall*

Silver gelatin print: *a black-and-white photograph taken with film*

Triptych: *an artwork made up of three panels*

EMERGING AND ESTABLISHED ARTISTS

When learning about an artist, you may hear them described as emerging, mid-career or established. This, as you might have guessed, is an indication of what stage an artist has reached in their career.

An emerging artist is someone at the beginning of their profession, whether they are straight out of art school or self-taught. It's not about age but experience. An emerging artist is likely to have just one collection of work to show, having recently caught the eye of a gallery or collector. You are most likely to find their work via art fairs and social media, both of which make it easy for you to chat with them and ask questions. One of the pleasures of buying from an emerging artist is the discovery of someone new. In buying their work, you are supporting them in their career, as well as hopefully being part of their journey to greater success.

A mid-career artist will have been working for at least five or 10 years and is likely to have a few collections of work under their belt by this time. They will have been exhibited in galleries locally and nationally and put on solo shows. Their pieces will have a recognizable style and, although they may not be painting full time, they will be doing so consistently. Mid-career artists make up the bulk of the artwork you will find in smaller bricks-and-mortar galleries as well as online spaces.

An established artist is someone who has a successful full-time career in the profession and may even be a household name. They will have exhibited and sold their work in prominent galleries both nationally and internationally and they regularly hold solo shows. Works by established artists will generally be on the more expensive end of the price scale.

POSTERS, PRINTS & ORIGINALS

When you buy a piece of art, it may be called a print (also known as a poster), a limited-edition print or an original. What are the differences between them?

A print or poster is machine-printed in the thousands or even hundreds of thousands, with no limitations on the number that can be made. It can be a reproduction of a famous artwork, such as Vincent Van Gogh's *Sunflowers*, or of a design by a little-known artist who has been commissioned to create a mass-market, inexpensive artwork. A print can also be made for a specific purpose, such as an exhibition poster sold as a souvenir.

A limited-edition print is a handmade original work that is made a set number of times (called an edition). The design can be made as a stencil, carved onto wood or linoleum or etched or engraved onto metal to create a block or template.

OPPOSITE LEFT Art and books always look good together. In this living room, volumes both stacked and upright are mixed in with art propped on the table to form an eye-catching tableau. Finishing the look is a Fornasetti plate on the wall with a twisting twig bringing the outside in.

OPPOSITE RIGHT The graphic design of this poster, *The Move At The Marquee 1967* by creative duo Hapshash and the Coloured Coat, adds brilliant colour and pattern hanging above the mantelpiece.

ABOVE LEFT The pink of the walls is picked up in this artwork by Alessandra Chambers from Partnership Editions – but with the addition of a mustard shade that introduces rich colour and complements the tones of the table and dining chairs.

ABOVE RIGHT A seascape photograph teamed with a black metal fireplace creates a modern look that suits the poured concrete floor of this room. At the same time, it is a strong visual contrast to the colour of the shelves and the textures of the soft furnishings.

ASK AN EXPERT:
Let's talk about style

Breaking art down into a style (often called genre) makes it easier to recognize the different looks you will come across when buying. "These categories are a good way of understanding what kinds of art you like," says Erica Davis of Murus Art.

Abstract: "An image that is undefined and more about a feeling and a mood rather than a representation of a specific thing or reference point. Abstract art is much more open to interpretation – you and the person standing next to you can see totally different things when looking at it."

Graphic: "There is a fine line between abstract and graphic art, but the latter has more structure to it with recognizable patterns and shapes."

Landscape: "A depiction of a countryside scene, whether it be hills or a beach. It can be of a particular place or one that combines the artist's memory and feelings for a landscape that is imaginary. Seascapes use the power of water to create a calming feeling – their colours give seascapes their own sense of escapism. Then there are cityscapes, urban scenes that can be identifiable or more abstract, conveying the mood of a particular city."

Still life: "A composition of objects, often food, drink, plants and flowers. One of the oldest art forms, it is now being reinterpreted by new and emerging artists in fun and quirky ways."

Botanical art: "A representation of flora as seen by an artist – not always a true representation of a particular plant or flower."

Figurative: "The study of the body, whether it be the face or torso. It can be quite specific or more abstracted but the focus is on the figure, either to make a comment or to transport you to a place and time."

RIGHT Matching the theme of an artwork to the function of a room is a great way of making it gel with the space. In this dining room, an acrylic and collage painting entitled *A Nice Juicy Pear* by Frankie Thorp from Murus Art adds cheering bright colour and a hint of playfulness, too.

BELOW Art can be a contrast to what's in the room or, as in this room, bring it all together. Here, a vintage French oil painting in a worn wooden frame complements the distressed state of the console table and the well-worn objects on it.

Three abstract artworks from Murus Art work as a set and pick up the colours found in the furniture and accessories of this living room, creating a space that feels cohesive and comfortable. At the top left is *Rudder* by Jonathan Lawes, with *Loopholes* by Marcus Aitken to the right and *Urban Life* by Iona Stern below.

This template is then used by the artist to handprint the design onto paper or canvas to create an original print. Each one is signed by the artist and marked with its edition number; for example, 5/100 means it was the fifth print to be created out of an edition of 100. An artist may make ten, 100 or 1,000, but when the last print is sold, it is gone. It is an accepted tradition in the art world that an artist will not make more than the original number stated, even if the demand is greater than expected. However, the total run does not have to be made all at once; as the process can be time-consuming, the artist will often stagger the run, returning to the template to make more when needed.

The limited-edition print *Loch with Dandelions* by Angie Lewin is the starting point of this pretty still-life arrangement on the shelf. The colours of the small bowls can be found in the painting, with the forest green adding freshness.

An artist can also make a series of "artist's proofs", which cannot number more than ten per cent of the total limited-edition run. These will be numbered "AP1", "AP2" and so on.

An original artwork is a one-off – the artist has created just one of it and it is the only one in existence. As artists have a distinctive and recognizable style, there may be other works that look similar, but the original artwork will never be replicated. The appeal of an original is that no-one else in the world will have what you have.

RIGHT A DIY artwork – a row of canvas blocks painted by Finnish designer Ulla Koskinen and in colours found throughout her home – is a simple but effective way of decorating a large wall.

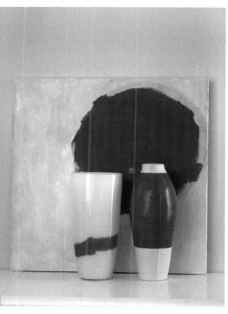

FAR LEFT & LEFT Art can be used to emphasize colour. In this living room, the painting by Julio Rondo on the mantelpiece is in the same shade of blue as the wall behind it (far left). Similarly, on a shelf, the vivid red of the glaze on the vases matches the richness of the colour in the painting (left).

ASK AN EXPERT:
Choosing photographs

Interested in photography for your walls? Art consultant Louisa Warfield explains what to look for.

Art in the home is all about creating a mood; if you're after a crisper, cooler finish to your space, then take a look at photography. Art consultant Louisa Warfield often incorporates photography when creating an art collection for clients. "Unlike a painting or print that has texture, a photograph is a flat image, so it brings something different to a room," she says. "It can make a traditional space feel more contemporary and also perfectly suits modern, loft-like spaces."

Photographs can be created using a variety of specialized processes, but the two most common forms are silver gelatin prints and digital prints. "Silver gelatin prints are the traditional form of photography," says Louisa. "A photographer shoots on film and the images are then developed in a dark room." Digital prints are the newer form that we are all familiar with thanks to smartphones and Instagram – the photographer takes the photograph digitally, then downloads the image to a computer. "They can then manipulate it by, for example, adding more colour or brightening some areas and darkening others, or collaging new images into the shot." For some photographers, silver gelatin prints are still the ultimate practice of their craft. However, this form is becoming increasingly rare, overtaken by the speed and lower costs that digital photography offers.

When choosing a photograph, what else should you look for? "The same as you would with any artwork," says Louisa: "strength of image, the composition and whether you connect to it in some way." You also need to pay particular attention to where the photograph is hung. "Photographs should always be shown behind glass – bear in mind that even non-reflective glass will show reflections unless you are standing directly in front of the photograph," says Louisa.

Photographs are often sold in editions, with each size having its own edition number. The smallest size may have an edition of 25, while a super-size may have been printed just once. The larger the print, the higher the price. "In some cases, an edition is priced flat, so the price for all the prints is the same,' says Louisa. "More often, though, the first few prints of an edition will be sold at a lower price to encourage sales."

ABOVE A black-and-white poster of a laughing Barack Obama as a young man injects energy into the room while maintaining the monochrome palette. The shape of Obama's hat is picked up in the lampshade.

RIGHT Photographs can be abstract, too. Here, a contemporary image hung low on the wall acts as a contrast to the kilim cushions/pillows. Together with the larger photograph propped on the floor, it gives the room a modern feel despite the traditional fabrics.

Size equals impact and the scale of this Josephine Alberthe photograph, printed on two panels, makes you feel as though you're in Kongens Have, a beautiful park in central Copenhagen. The muted colours are warmer than black and white, but not so bright that they jar with the quiet metallic tones of the room.

WHAT GIVES AN ARTWORK ITS VALUE?

Putting a price on a piece of art is an inexact science, as art is so subjective – one person may love a painting that leaves someone else completely cold. However, an artwork's value generally comes down to combination of factors.

Firstly, the artist and what stage they are in their career. Works by artists who have a track record of sales and strong demand will be worth more. Past sale prices will also be a useful guide. Emerging artists are far more difficult to predict. Thanks to social media, which allows them to sell directly to the public, many will launch with a price that is testing the water and change it over time.

The materials used can also affect the price. For example, charcoal and paper are fairly low-cost, so an artwork created using them will have a lower starting price than one made with more expensive materials such as resin.

Finally, the type of artwork will also come into play. Original artworks, being one of a kind, will have a higher starting value. Limited-edition prints and artist's proofs, which are signed and finite in number, will be valued more highly than a mass-produced poster. However, posters made for past exhibitions by famous artists may have value. Even if they are not limited editions, only a certain number will have been made for the exhibition and they will no longer be easily available.

OPPOSITE A room doesn't need to be saturated with colour for it to make an impression. In this almost all-white space, the yellow of the artwork really stands out, adding warmth, but also a happy vibe. The mustard-coloured pouffe gives balance to the colour scheme so that the art doesn't feel out of step.

ABOVE These three artworks complement the deep shade of blue on the walls. The framed work is by David Shrigley and the puddle sculpture on the floor (just visible through the legs of the table) is by art group A Kassen. A neon blue piece by Gun Gordillo adds an electric touch that enlivens the room.

ASK AN EXPERT:
Get that vintage vibe

Vintage art is an affordable and popular art choice. Sara Allom, founder of The Vintage Art Gallery, defines its appeal.

Vintage art is a popular way to start a collection without breaking the bank, but the nostalgic appeal of a faded landscape or an unknown portrait goes beyond affordability. "It's about connecting to precious memories," says Sara Allom. "Someone will look at a painting of a beach, for example, and be reminded of their childhood holidays by the sea. Or with a portrait, the sitter's dress might be similar to one owned by a much-loved relative."

Sara's website is a specialist online emporium where you can browse all kinds of preloved paintings and prints. There is no period that defines a vintage artwork, but the most common styles are landscapes, seascapes, still lifes and portraits. The majority are painted in oils. "You rarely know who painted them," says Sara, "but the mystery is part of the attraction. I find a vintage work will always spark a conversation."

She only chooses pieces that have artistic merit, though their charm is not just about the talent of the painter. "There is a texture to vintage art that is beautiful," says Sara. "The colours cannot be replicated today because the oil paints were made in a different way at that time. Similarly, vintage prints have a patina and tone that you can't buy now – this authenticity gives them value."

This sense of age and history makes vintage art particularly effective at giving homes a sense of permanence and belonging. "It's an affordable way of introducing a second-hand piece into a new home, making it feel less shiny and new," says Sara.

Vintage art can be bought from speciality sellers such as Sara or sourced in antique stores, markets and car boot sales. Paintings and prints usually come framed, but don't be afraid to change the frame. "Just make sure you choose a frame that has an aged feel or a vintage shape so the artwork retains its authentic feel."

OPPOSITE ABOVE A vintage still life, with faded colours that give it a particular charm, is the starting point for a collection of curiosities in a variety of shapes and textures.

OPPOSITE BELOW The symmetry of the decoration in this room has been carefully thought out. The antiques stand out within the modern white space, but also within themselves have a mix of straight lines and curvy shapes. The stool, portrait and ornaments have a palette of yellow and brown tones that fit in with the gold accents on the chandelier above.

ABOVE The shabby-chic look of this living room is accentuated by the vintage art, which also adds subtle colour and a feeling of comfort. The pale pinks and blues of the floral still life are balanced by the subdued greens of the landscape over the mantelpiece and by the greenery outside.

RIGHT A large black-and-white vintage portrait is a foil to the brown and cream tones of the antique cabinet and decorative objects that sit on top of it. However, the brown wooden frame brings it into the composition as a striking focal point.

FAMILY HISTORY

The walls of Sandra Barrio von Hurter's home are filled with art that tells a story.

Sandra Barrio von Hurter describes the art on her walls as "a collection of memories" and it's true that it reflects the people and places that she and her husband Felix love. "Each piece has a story behind it, and that's how we like it," she says. Sandra, who works as a jewellery designer, was born in Barcelona and moved to London more than a decade ago. "We buy prints from the exhibitions we go to and we buy art when we travel so that we have memories of where we have been," she continues. "It could be a hand-painted postcard, a piece of wood that has been painted, an amazing photograph or a ceramic. We also love to display gifts we have been given, such as an old map of the Greek island on which we were married."

The couple's art tells the stories of their families, too. "The large painting in the living room was the first piece of art my parents-in-law bought when they were living in New York," says Sandra. "Above their flat lived a painter and they bought the painting from him for $100, which was very expensive then. It hung in their London home for years and I always loved it. When we moved here, they gifted it to us." The black-and-white printed pub mirrors were bought by Sandra's father more than 50 years ago when he borrowed his grandfather's Fiat 600 and travelled to London on holiday at the age of 18. "When I moved to London, he gave me five of them, which are dotted around the house," she says.

Much of the art is bold and bright, which chimes with the colours on the walls of the four-bedroom house. As an antidote to London's often grey skies, Sandra and Felix turned to paint to give their Victorian home cheering colour, settling on

OPPOSITE The international art in the kitchen includes, from left, a poster of Diego Rivera's *The Day of the Dead* from Mexico, an original work from an Athens market and a Messias Neiva painting from a Brazilian charity auction.

ABOVE In daughter Frida's room, colourful letters on the mantel echo the hues of the print above: *A Sea Picnic* by children's author and illustrator Edith Farmiloe.

shades found in nature such as olive and sage greens, mustard yellow, nasturtium orange and pale pink. "And because we love colour, our art is colourful too; it's an extension of ourselves and our tastes," she says.

In the kitchen, deep red Picasso prints are hung as a gallery wall. "They're posters that he drew advertising bullfights in France," says Sandra. "They were in an old book that fell apart and I chose the colourful ones and put them together. I did something similar in my daughter Frida's bathroom using pages from an old book on Mexican dresses that I loved."

These clever ways of turning the simplest things into impactful art mean the walls are never bare. "This is a big house, and we don't have the money to spend big," says Sandra. "But it's possible if you follow your taste and you're not scared to mix things together and think differently about what art is."

"EACH PIECE HAS A STORY BEHIND IT, AND THAT'S HOW WE LIKE IT."

LEFT Sandra and Felix's art comes in variety of styles and frames. On the far left is a poster from a Frida Kahlo exhibition held at London's Victoria & Albert Museum. On the right of the wall-mounted plate rack is a print of Hôtel Le Gallic in Dinard, northern France, by C Bullock; next to it is an original landscape bought on a trip to Peru.

ABOVE In the dining area, Sandra created a striking gallery wall by framing pages from a 1964 book of artist Pablo Picasso's posters, which he created to advertise bullfights in the French town of Vallauris. The black and red frames add extra colour and complement the art without overpowering it.

LEFT & BELOW Two black-and-white artworks mounted on the living room shelves help to break up the mass of books (left). The one on the left is by Oriol Aribau; on the right is a drawing by Alexandria Coe. Above the mantelpiece, a focal point in this room, hangs a framed headdress from the indigenous Kayapo people of Brazil that was given to the couple as a wedding gift (below). The white of the headdress accentuated by the dark mount/mat presents a visual contrast to the rich green colour of the painted bookshelves.

OPPOSITE Another focal point in the living room is above the sofa, where an enormous oil painting by an unknown artist hangs on the wall. It was gifted to the couple by Felix's parents. Large in scale and brightly coloured, it dominates the room but doesn't overwhelm the headdress on the opposite wall.

OPPOSITE On the eclectic gallery wall in Sandra's office, a Jean Dubuffet exhibition poster hangs above a copy of Marlene Dumas's *The Image as Burden*. In the centre, next to a Brad Elterman photograph of the wrap party for *Grease*, is a reproduction of David Shrigley's *Elephant Chooses to Stand on Your Car*. In the small red frame is an original by Laetitia Rouget. Paintings on wood from Morocco and ceramics from Brazil add textural interest.

LEFT & BELOW LEFT The James Dean pub mirror on the staircase wall is part of a collection that once belonged to Sandra's father (left). An oil painting by Linda Sutton entitled *Rhinoceros on exhibition in Venice* was a gift from Felix's parents. The fruit vase on the mantelpiece below was made by Sandra.

BELOW Leading up from the ground floor, the staircase gallery wall is made up of a mix of black-and-white and colour museum prints along with pieces of sentimental value. In a variety of frames, together they create a relaxed look.

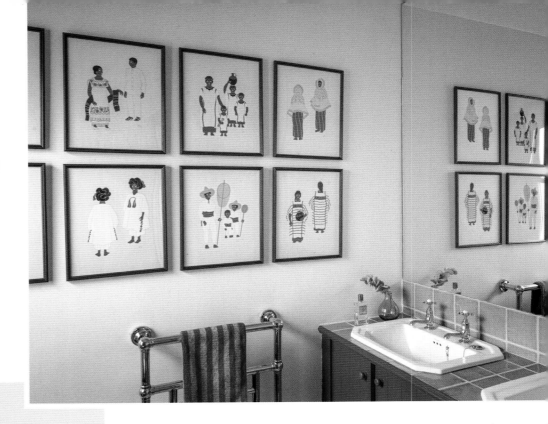

RIGHT Pages from a favourite old book on Mexican dresses have been framed to create a gallery wall in Frida's bathroom. The plain wooden frames and grid arrangement create a striking effect, the colours also tying in nicely with the tones of the bathroom furnishings.

ART NOTES

What's the story behind the Carla Llanos prints in your bedroom?

"We built up a relationship over Instagram. I loved her art and she loved my jewellery, so we did a creative exchange!"

How did you do the gallery walls in your stairwell?

"I wanted the two walls to be different, so the wall along the first flight of stairs is a mix of paintings, exhibition prints, drawings by a friend and similar artworks. The wall on the second flight of stairs is all family photographs, a mix of old ones and new, and all framed in black."

What's your one piece of advice?

"Not all walls need to look like an 'art wall'. I wanted our bedroom to be calm and serene, so I chose to have a less-is-more style that contrasts with the rest of the house. We went for more bare walls and art with a lighter colour palette."

RIGHT Above the bed in the spare bedroom, the focal point of the space, hangs a print of *Mountain Landscape, Majorca* by Frederick Gore. The vibrant colours of the room are reflected in the print, including the deep orange of the wall behind it.

OPPOSITE Instead of competing with the highly decorative antique headboard in the main bedroom by hanging art above the bed, Sandra instead placed it on either side, above the bedside tables. Positioned partway down the side of the bed at eye level, this print by Carla Llanos feels balanced.

"I WANTED OUR BEDROOM TO BE CALM AND SERENE, SO I CHOSE TO HAVE A LESS-IS-MORE STYLE."

VASE 04
Serie Cerámica | Carla 1

NATURAL BEAUTY

A love of nature inspires the art found in
the home of garden designer Dorthe Kvist.

ABOVE Wooden boxes in different sizes have been
put together to create a square and filled with a mix
of houseplants and decorative objects in shades of
green and white. They make an engaging display
that adds interest to a corner.

Dorthe Kvist's home is a great example of how one's taste in
art can change when one's life enters a new phase. A couple
of years ago, this was a modern and pared-back space with
bold, abstract paintings taking centre stage. Today, though,
furniture in floral prints is complemented by botanical
artworks for a softer, more boho mood.

What brought about this change? "I worked in the fashion
business for 18 years and then I became a garden designer,"
says Dorthe. "My style nowadays is wilder, more natural
and uncontrolled and my home reflects this. Now I can't get
enough of botany!" In one corner of the living room, where
once a graphic print was coolly propped on a metal shelf
unit, there's now a wooden bench and above it, a gallery wall
featuring images of dried seed pods. "I find them beautiful
and for me, they also possess great poetry," says Dorthe.

Dorthe, who shares her home in Denmark with husband
Jakob and their two children, is a magpie when it comes to
finding art, picking up pieces she loves from markets, online
galleries and exhibitions. One particularly eye-catching piece
is a poster of an artwork by Walton Ford, the American artist
known for his dynamic natural history paintings. "I bought it
from my favourite gallery, the Louisiana Museum of Modern
Art in Humlebæk, which is not far from where I live," says
Dorthe. "I have visited this museum since my childhood, and
I love it. It's located at a very beautiful spot right on the coast,
with a huge, beautiful garden around it."

Another much-loved poster is from the University of
Copenhagen Botanical Garden. "It's a place I visit as often as
I can – the poster shows the beautiful palm house, which was
built in the 1870s," says Dorthe. "Made of cast iron and glass,
it was inspired by Crystal Palace in London."

Above a sideboard/credenza in an adjoining room is an
interesting mix of art including a black-and-white painting
and drawings bought at a Christmas market at the School
of Architecture in Copenhagen. "Also included is a poster
of Yoko Ono, who is a great inspiration to me, and the 'S'
is because Jakob's surname is Sørensen," says Dorthe. "I put
the pieces side by side because their colours and energy work
together. For me, art is a natural part of my decor, and just
as important as furniture, colour and plants. And as a kind
of artist in my work as a garden designer, I know how many
emotions and thoughts can lie behind a piece of art."

In her second living room, Dorthe has combined wood with monochrome art for a modern boho look. The gallery wall includes a small, graphic painting by Anna Sørensen and a poster of Yoko Ono, a heroine of Dorthe's, from a retrospective at Denmark's Louisiana Museum of Modern Art. The objects on the sideboard/credenza, along with the branch and hanging plant, bring the look together.

PAGE 38 A diverse mix of objects comes together to create an eye-catching display in the main living room with a colour palette defined by the vintage oil painting, which Dorthe inherited from her mother. Above, trailing foliage and framed dried flowers add to the botanical theme.

PAGE 39 A large artwork by Anna Sørensen adds colour and a happy vibe to this room, while a blanket bought when Dorthe was in Vietnam warms a rattan chair. A green figure on the windowsill ties in with the green of the houseplants.

OPPOSITE & LEFT Floral upholstery, houseplants and vases of flowers set a botanical mood in the living room, accentuated by the artwork. The arresting poster is of a Walton Ford artwork, *Baba*. On another wall is a poster showing the 19th-century palm house at the University of Copenhagen Botanical Garden, one of Dorthe's favourite places to visit.

ABOVE In the dining room, long shelves in the same white as the wall bring decoration into the room. Stacked books, spines facing outwards, add colour and are a foil to the monochrome art above.

Dorthe has made what could have been a neglected corner of the room interesting with a mix of images of dried seedpods along with botanical drawings. The lime-green string of the hanging pots adds a pop of vibrancy.

BELOW In the bedroom, a small black-and-white artwork, hung off centre above the bed, invites a closer look. Paper spheres suspended from the ceiling anchor the artwork, so that it doesn't feel lost on the large expanse of wall.

"FOR ME, ART IS A NATURAL PART OF MY DECOR, AND JUST AS IMPORTANT AS FURNITURE, COLOUR AND PLANTS."

ART NOTES

Which artwork do you have the strongest emotional connection with?
"The oil painting that is displayed on the wooden shelves in my living room. I inherited it from my late mother, who won it in a raffle at her work, and I was so happy to be given it. My mother lived in the town of Hornbæk on the northern coast of Denmark, close to the beach, and the painting could easily have been painted there, so it reminds me of her and of Hornbæk."

How do you decide where to hang an artwork?
"I hang it where I think it contributes the right energy to the particular room. Art can set a mood, can lead to reflection, to inspiration and to conversations that can often end up in very interesting places; I choose to hang an artwork depending on what mood I want the room to have and how I want to feel when I am in it."

What advice would you give to people buying art?
"A piece of art must be chosen with the heart and evoke emotions, whether it's a ceramic, photograph, painting or whatever it may be. So don't think about the monetary value, but choose with your heart and with your eyes."

HOW TO START
A COLLECTION

f you haven't bought art before, how do you begin? Before we go on, the first thing to say is that there are no rules about choosing art; there is no right or wrong, good taste or bad.

Choosing an artwork can often make us feel nervous – am I choosing the right kind of artwork? What does it say about me that I like this work but someone else doesn't? Does it mean I have terrible taste? The short answer is no, because it is enough that you love the piece of art and feel connected to it in some way. Perhaps it's the colours or the patterns within it, the scene that takes you back to a time and place or a memory that no one else shares. Similarly, don't be afraid to say that you don't like something or that you feel nothing for it.

So, how do you start buying art? There are two ways of doing so. The first is instinctively – you're buying the artwork because you love it. It may be that you see a work and feel you must have it, whether you find it online or on your travels. Then it's a matter of bringing it home and deciding where it best fits. The second is more practical – you're after an artwork to hang in a specific place in your home. It can be tricky envisaging how the artwork will look in a room, especially as you're most likely to first see it set against a white background, but you can start by thinking about size and colour (see more on this on page 48).

That said, even if you're buying practically rather than instinctively, you still need to like the artwork, otherwise seeing it every day will give you little joy. In time, it may even come to irritate you. So don't be tempted to buy something just because it's trending or painted by a cool artist everyone is raving about – buy it because you really like what you see.

And most importantly, take your time. The art collections that are most enjoyable to look at have usually been put together over a long period with pieces collected from a variety of places including flea markets, art fairs, galleries and shops.

PAGES 44–45 In this bright, relaxed room, pressed flowers create visually arresting and textured art alongside paintings by Annemiek de Beer and Andrea Letterie.

OPPOSITE These photographic prints are all from ArtStar. *Light Up I* by Carla Sutera Sardo livens up a corner (above left). William Wegman's *B is for Baker* lends character (above right). *Alive* and *Something Just Like This* by Tom Fabia take us outdoors (below).

QUESTION TIME

When Chrissy Crawford, founder of the online platform ArtStar, plans art for a room, she considers the person living in it so she can match the art to their personality and situation. These are the types of questions she asks her clients.

"Live in the city but crave nature?
Choose images of trees, flowers and other greenery to bring the outside in."

"Does your room lack windows or an uplifting view?
A landscape photograph that mimics a vista might be just the thing."

"Need your space to make you feel relaxed and rested?
You don't have to live at the beach to have coastal images on your walls. In soft, pastel colours, they're wonderfully calming."

"Love to travel?
Do so from your sofa or bed with images from around the world. And if you've been to a destination, seeing it in your art will bring back great memories."

"Not a morning person?
A fun image that makes you smile is the perfect way to kick-start the day."

"Need a Zoom background?
Pick something with colour, but not too busy. It should make a statement, but not detract from the conversation."

"Decorating your child's room?
What are they into – sports, dance, dolls? Try to match their interests, but look for art that is not too juvenile so that they won't outgrow it."

BUY WHAT YOU LOVE

It's easy to say "buy what you love", but how exactly do you go about figuring out what you like and what you don't? How do you narrow down the enormous choice that's available?

One thing you definitely should not do is head to your closest gallery or switch on your laptop and start browsing with the intention of buying something there and then. Instead, take the time to look at a variety of artworks in stores, online and in bricks-and-mortar galleries, and via social media. Consider different styles, eras and mediums, as well as subject matter.

Think about how each individual piece makes you feel. In particular, consider what styles of art you are drawn to. Do you respond to pithy words that inspire you or make you laugh, do you love landscapes that let you mentally escape into the countryside or are you a fan of abstracts that encourage you to daydream and switch off? Equally, is there a type of artwork that you really dislike? Once you have an idea of the types of art that appeals to you, you will feel much more confident in your taste, which in turn makes it easier to buy what you really love.

GO BIG OR GO SMALL?

Decorating your home with art means mixing large and small pieces, each of which has a different role to play in styling a room. A large statement artwork is one that sits on a wall on its own and is a natural focal point in a room. Its sheer size also means it significantly influences, and even dictates, the mood of the space it is in.

A work that is full of colour and drama will create an energetic and vibrant feel, whereas one with a more muted colour palette will promote a relaxed atmosphere. Deciding

on the mood you want for a room is a good starting place when choosing a large artwork. However, this rule can apply differently in a maximalist space that you have already filled with brightly coloured furniture, bookshelves and ornaments. In this kind of room, even a statement artwork, if full of fine details, can lose its impact. Instead, choose an artwork with large-scale motifs – anything more intricate will be better suited to a more pared-back space where it can truly stand out.

Smaller artworks are never going to be a focal point on their own, but they're perfect for adding a finishing touch or bringing interest to a space that might otherwise be overlooked. Easy to find a space for, they are also the perfect impulse buy, as they're small enough to find a home among your exisiting collection. They're also versatile, allowing you to change up a room easily and quickly.

OPPOSITE LEFT Textiles draped over a beautiful loveseat introduce red, yellow and orange tones, with the latter also found in the modern abstract painting by Sandra Whitmore that hangs above.

OPPOSITE RIGHT A vintage sign, in keeping with the seaside theme, brings a smile to the face and acts as the main piece of art in this bedroom. Corals and starfish are displayed on the shelf below.

ABOVE LEFT Bold patterned wallpaper is the background for a pair of bird prints in matching frames. The coloured mount/mat echoes the shade of green found in the prints. A total style contrast to the wallpaper, they immediately catch the eye.

ABOVE RIGHT A large painting by Sara Schmidt is part of an eclectically styled space in her home that also includes a chest and vintage folding chairs.

IN THE MOOD

When choosing where to hang an existing artwork or deciding on a new purchase, you can either reflect the colour palette of the room in which you plan to hang it or make a statement by choosing colours that are different.

It is far easier to choose an artwork whose colours are similar to the room decor, so if you're not confident working with colour, then this is the way forward. Choose a painting that features the same colour tones (or variations of them) that are found in the room; for example, if you have a deep green sofa, ensure a similar green is in the artwork. Alternatively, opt for the accent shades such as those found in a rug, cushions or other textiles. If you do want to make a statement with your artwork by choosing colours that are not in the existing decor, you can make the process easier by using a colour wheel to decide on complementary colours that work well together, such as red and green or blue and orange.

Deciding on the mood you would like to create in a room is a good starting point when selecting the style of art you would like to have in it. Would you like the space to feel elegant or relaxed, dramatic or soothing, light and bright or warm and cosy? Although there are no rules on what style of art should be in which room, there are some spaces in the home that lend themselves to one particular vibe over others, as you will see on the following pages.

OPPOSITE A photograph by Barry Cawston propped on a Victorian-era mantel combines old and new. Framed in white, and with pared-back styling on either side, the work stands out against the mustard walls and reflects the other colours found in the space.

ABOVE In the dining area of this maximalist apartment, pinks and greens abound. A strong contrast in style to the wallpaper behind, but in the same palette as the room, is a photograph of supermodel Kate Moss taken by Ellen von Unwerth.

RIGHT An artwork from the series called *Black Antoinette* by Olaf Hajek makes what could be an uninteresting space between kitchen cupboards into an area that is full of character.

ASK AN EXPERT:
Keeping to a budget

*Georgia Spray, founder of Partnership Editions,
explains how to buy with a budget in mind.*

Whether you've renovated your home and would now like
to fill it with art, or you have a budget that you plan to spend
over time, how do you allocate it so you don't run out of
money before you've finished? "Ask yourself what are the
key spaces in your home and consider spending more of your
budget there," advises Georgia Spray of Partnership Editions.
She founded the online platform for emerging artists and
collectors with the aim of making art more affordable.

In Georgia's experience, the living room is always an
important area of the home for art and therefore worth
spending a good proportion of your budget on. "Having a large
artwork above a sofa or mantelpiece makes quite an impact,"
she says, "and although it might feel like a big investment in
one work, you can then be more playful in other nooks around
your house – above side tables or in alcoves. Decorate these
spaces with posters and more affordable artwork."

As large works usually cost more than smaller ones, "figure out
what you can afford to spend and then look for the types of art
that are more likely to fit your budget," says Georgia. This may
mean a limited-edition print rather than an original painting,
or opting for a photograph or a piece of vintage art. And don't
forget about the frame. "People often don't realise that framing
is expensive, so you need to budget that in as well," explains
Georgia. "If you have a large artwork to be framed behind art
glass, that can cost even more than the work of art itself."

Once you've decided on your spend in the living room, apply
this same approach to your other rooms. Take into account
the conditions in the room, too. If you would like art in the
bathroom, it may be be better to display an inexpensive poster,
as an original artwork runs the risk of being ruined by steam.

The gallery wall is a much-loved option, but you need to think
carefully before you start spending. "They can actually add
up to be a lot more expensive than one large piece once you've
factored in multiple artworks plus their framing costs," Georgia
says. It may be that you need to start small with your gallery
wall, kicking it off with a handful of pieces and adding to it
over time as your budget allows.

ABOVE A still life of objects creates a tranquil mood.
The vintage artwork combined with a Picasso print are
accessorized with pots and plants, while a glass table lamp
adds another material into the mix. Together, they make
the very different art styles look cohesive.

OPPOSITE BELOW
This corner of an open-plan living space is styled up with a console, above which a mix of artworks is casually displayed. One is simply stuck to the wall, another attached with a paper clip. The festoon lights act as an enormous frame.

THIS PAGE An abstract painting by Duncan Pickstock gives this living room a real sense of calm. In a soft colour palette of blue and grey that ties in with the walls and soft furnishings, it helps pull the space together without overly dominating it.

LIVING ROOMS

The living room is such a varied space. It can be a single room or part of an open-plan living area. It can be enjoyed in so many ways, whether it is a place to relax quietly with a book, watch television or have fun with family and friends. All of which means that the living room lends itself to a variety of different styles, depending on the feeling you want in the room. For a space in which the dominant mood is relaxation, choose a soothing abstract artwork or a peaceful landscape. For a greater sense of energy, use bolder colours and graphic prints to lend a room vibrancy. You can also use art to add a touch of playfulness, choosing works that make you smile.

RIGHT This living room skilfully combines different styles, from the traditional cabinets to the contemporary armchairs and vases on the tray table. A painting by Jette Segnitz captures the colours of the space on a single canvas, stylishly pulling the room together.

OPPOSITE Full of colour and life, this artwork is actually a scarf by Helen Dealtry – its design was inspired by ikebana, the Japanese art of flower arranging. It is large enough to be the only decoration needed on the main wall of the living room.

ABOVE Artist Claire Basler displays her large, expressive paintings of flowers throughout her home. Instead of being hung, these two are simply propped on a shelving unit that wraps around the radiator. The relaxed form of display lends the room a laid-back feel.

RIGHT *Belong Red Cedar*, a multimedia artwork made of mulberry-fibre paper and wood by Tsuyu, holds pride of place in this living room. The natural materials add a sense of warmth while suiting the contemporary look of the space.

ABOVE LEFT A portrait by Ian Webb is finished with a distressed frame, which suits the style and finish of the artwork. Together they fit the rustic design of the space.

ABOVE CENTRE A print of *Les Cheveux Courts* by Kees van Dongen hangs in a corner with a vintage landscape propped on the mahogany side table below it, the similar frames linking the two. The red resin table lamp adds a shot of colour.

ABOVE RIGHT A collage of images creates a striking artwork, the busyness a foil to the pared-back style of the fireplace but corresponding to the variety of colours in the room.

LEFT The blue-grey tones of the walls are a near perfect match for one of the colours in the artwork by Tom Humphreys, and the colour-blocking style reflects the way the room has been styled. A bright frame accentuates the piece.

A vintage oil painting hung from the picture frame in an ornate gilt frame, the latter glowing softly against the pink walls, complements the panelling of this historic house. However, the room feels modern thanks to the contemporary sofa and floor lamp.

ABOVE LEFT An eye-catching print makes a statement in this living room, the glittery pink and close-up framing of the image immediately grabbing the attention. It is a playful contrast to the more elegant style of the space.

OPPOSITE BELOW A vintage scarf by Richard Allan is mounted and framed to create a piece of art that fits the mid-century modern feel of the room. The curvy shapes of the scarf are reflected in the vases and ornaments on the sideboard/credenza.

ABOVE A large black-and-white fashion print commands the room, in contrast with the colour around it. The compact gallery wall plays with balance with two images hung at different heights within the width of the pink sofa and a third overhanging slightly.

KITCHENS &
DINING ROOMS

These are rooms in which to have
some fun. Pop Art-style works that
show typical kitchen products such as
ketchup bottles and canned foodstuffs
fit well here, together with pieces in
which life imitates art, such as still
lifes of fruit bowls and table settings.
If your kitchen cabinets are neutral,
artworks in bright colours are a stylish
way to introduce a pop of colour.

OPPOSITE Breaking with the traditional kitchen look of fitted cabinets means there is space to hang a piece of art above the sink. The daffodils here add a gorgeous splash of colour and joy in this boho warehouse apartment.

ABOVE In this dining area, which is decorated predominantly in tones of white and brown, two graphic limited-edition prints by German sculptor Friedrich Gräsel add energy and help to zone the space by creating a focal point. Both prints are untitled; the one on the left dates from 1968 and the other from 1967.

ABOVE RIGHT A still life of a tablescape is a perfect fit for a kitchen or dining area and this painting by Lise Eriksen with its many details really elevates the space. An arrangement of tableware on a cake stand in front of the artwork is a charming touch.

RIGHT A series of small, brightly hued images arranged in a stepped pattern creates a gallery wall display that invites the viewer to take a closer look. The images are mounted/matted and framed in a variety of ways, but the strength of the colours creates a cohesive look.

RIGHT The layers of interest on the wall of this kitchen make it a beautiful space to be in. The vintage paintings and old French confit pots on a shelf add subtle colour and character. Together with the hanging utensils, they make for a traditional contrast with the Shaker-style cabinets.

BELOW A Lucy Augé artwork featuring the delicacy of leaves and branches is a stunning focal point above the bench, standing out against the pale pink walls. The striped cushions/pillows inject cheery colour.

BELOW Art doesn't have to complicated or expensive. In this kitchen, a floral print in tones that complement the neutral palette of the wood panelling and ceramic vessels has been left unframed for a simple but effective display.

An abundance of nature fills this kitchen and dining space, the large floral artwork adding vibrancy to what would have been a sizeable expanse of white wall. Although the sofa is upholstered in a fabric that has a different mood, the styles are both bold enough that the clash works.

OFFICES

A variety of different art styles fit an office and, again, what you choose depends on how you want the artwork to make you feel. An abstract piece can create a peaceful space in which to sit and think while you wait for inspiration to strike. Botanical pieces bring a sense of the outside in, giving a connection to nature that also creates a restful mood. For a more empowering vibe, a graphic print with inspirational words can be effective, helping you to power on when faced with a challenge.

BELOW The white designer desk (by Bertjan Pot for Moooi) with its modern white accessories are a contrast to the surrounding vibrant colour provided by the books, Moroccan rug and bold artworks, including the striking dot painting by Warlpiri artist Lorna Fencer Napurrula.

OPPOSITE Floating shelves have been put in place above the desk, creating space to prop a series of inspiring images. The upper ledge is shorter than the lower one, with the stepped effect creating a more open look. Mostly monochrome in colour, the prints match the pared-back mood of the space.

ABOVE In this rustic monochrome space, a pair of prints in plain black frames, hung symmetrically, is the finishing touch. The colours in the prints reflect those in the room, from the flooring to the wall colour. Furniture and accessories in a soft off-white complete the scheme.

LEFT In this large dining and work space, an enormous portrait in a black frame is a cool full stop to the long table. The room is a mix of styles, but the art manages to work with all of them seamlessly.

BELOW LEFT Green and orange are the accent colours in this stylish office and both are reflected in the art. The wide, black mount/mat and matching frame accentuate the small green and white artwork, while the landscape benefits from an orange frame.

BELOW Large artworks – by Elon Brasil (left) and Duncan Pickstock (right) – make for a characterful space. The colours of both are found elsewhere in the room, so despite being of different styles, they do not clash or fight for attention.

OPPOSITE The red and orange of the canvases, bought from a street vendor in New York, complement the brick wall on which they hang. The combination unites a range of tones in this bright colour palette and gives this pared-back space a shot of zing.

LEFT A beautiful, contemplative artwork – a multi-exposed still of a mountainscape by Richard Friend – is a contrast to the busy wallpaper behind it, introducing a sense of tranquillity to this home office. The red chairs, although bright, draw the eye to the painting rather than detract from it.

OPPOSITE Between the propped monochrome poster and the framed print, black washi tape has been used to create a decorative faux frame that visually connects the two artworks. The decorative pieces on the ledge are in more earthy colours, injecting warmth into the black-and-white scheme.

RIGHT The yellow of the front door is introduced subtly in the entrance of this cottage with an abstract landscape in colours that hint at the front door shade as well as the darker hues found within. Framed in white, the art stands out against the dark walls, lightening the space. Entitled *April Pond*, it is by Seán McSweeney.

HALLWAYS

Not just a space to walk through, hallways with art can be well worth lingering in and set the tone for the rest of your home; after all, it's the first place you and your guests see when walking through the front door. Stop people in their tracks with an artwork that grabs the attention such as an abstract or graphic work in bright colours or stand-out pattern. Or, if you have a style or theme running through your home, feature it in your hallway as an introduction to your home. Take the size of your hallway into account when choosing. If it's not a large space, then too many works could make it feel cluttered – save the gallery wall for somewhere else.

BEDROOMS

As your bedroom is a personal space that you don't share with visitors, it's here that you can comfortably experiment with art that is different and is particularly personal to you. The primary function of a bedroom, though, is to help you relax and get a restful night's sleep, so loud artworks that fill the room with energy are usually best avoided. Instead, opt for art that is calming and escapist – botanical prints work well, as do landscapes, seascapes and abstract art in muted colours or combined with diluted pops of colour. Line drawings that are gestural and not too realistic or regimented also suit a bedroom.

The sloping ceiling and limited space make large-scale artworks impossible to hang in this bedroom. Instead, a compact gallery wall made of small but interesting art and decorative pieces, all in a natural colour palette, decorate the narrow wall.

RIGHT Bedside tables aren't just for books. In this bedroom, a lovely vintage painting propped against the wall is the starting point of a pretty display, with the light, pitcher and stack of books all echoing the pink and green tones found within the artwork.

ABOVE An unusual wallpaper, installed by a previous homeowner in the 1940s, creates a lovely textured look on the walls of this bedroom. A vintage landscape adds an uplifting splash of colour.

RIGHT The textured brick walls are a contrast to the shades of grey that are predominant colours in this room. However, the tones of the large triptych, by Elle Luna, soften the effect of the bricks. Soft pinks elsewhere connect the two.

RIGHT An abstract painting hung behind the headboard decorates the main wall, but the stars of the show are artworks by family members hung vertically above the bedside table. Although in different styles and frames, they come together for a fun, casual look.

LEFT A large floral painting by Claire Basler acts as a rather splendid headboard in this bedroom and appears almost framed by the four-poster bed. The deep blue walls both complement and accentuate the colours of the painting, making the flowers pop.

OPPOSITE A gallery wall featuring vintage paintings on a boating theme simply but stylishly decorates the wall behind the bed. The vintage theme continues in the room with the rustic stools as bedside tables, the pair of Anglepoise lamps and the patchwork quilt.

ABOVE LEFT To create their own distinctive wallpaper, the owners of this bathroom blew up sheet music by Ira Gershwin and treated it with a raw umber pigment to soften the starkness of the white, as well as a gel medium to make it waterproof.

ABOVE CENTRE Framed antique maps hung between panels give this bathroom unusual colours and shapes for a display that adds character.

ABOVE RIGHT White tiled walls can feel cold and stark. In this bathroom, warmth has been added with vintage artwork, a seascape and sailor keeping the theme appropriately water-based. The cane table and houseplant anchor the display so the artwork doesn't look like it's floating.

LEFT With the panelling painted in a heritage-style shade of green and a clawfoot tub, this bathroom has a traditional feel. The vintage portrait painting fits right in both in appearance and colour.

OPPOSITE This bathroom unites rustic and modern textures. On the traditional side are tadelakt walls, old shutters and a beaded wall hanging. Anchoring the latter is a contemporary stool, which complements the smooth curves of the modern free-standing bathtub.

BATHROOMS

Bathrooms are tricky spaces for art due to moisture in the air, so it's best to avoid hanging your most expensive works here. Canvas can withstand steaminess better than paper, and if you choose a framed print, make sure it is professionally framed to keep moisture out. Seascapes, with their link to water, are a good fit in a bathroom, as are abstracts that encourage you to drift off and grab a few moments of mindfulness, even if you're just brushing your teeth. Whimsical photographs are another possibility.

ABOVE A set of alphabet flashcards by Lisa DeJohn creates a wonderful block of colour and images that prettily decorates a focal wall of a child's room.

ABOVE RIGHT Framed black-and-white family photos are propped on the top ledge of a painted wooden shelf unit, along with a set of books and a collection of infant shoes, some standing and others hanging from their laces. It is a still life full of lovely details.

RIGHT A map of the world covers a wall of these twin toddlers' room, adding stimulating colour that balances the bright toys and books on the shelves. Over time, it will also have educational value and foster an interest in the wider world.

OPPOSITE A poster of a yawning hippo (the original was done by Sven Brasch for Copenhagen Zoo in 1924) and a cute Noodoll poster are an eclectic art combination that fits right in with the mix of fun objects in the room.

CHILDREN'S ROOMS

Choose art that stimulates ideas and creativity; it can be just for fun or educational, or a mix of the two. Alphabet-style art, for example, will help young children learn their letters while maps can prompt a curiosity about the world. Children love colour, so artworks in bright shades will catch their interest as well as give the room a cheery feel.

DARK STAR

Catherine Ashton thought carefully about the art she chose for her almost-black walls. The result is a home that is full of character.

The dark and moody walls of Catherine Ashton's two-bedroom apartment make a wonderful backdrop for her extensive collection of art, the pieces coming together to create a home that is full of character and style.

Her distinctive look begins as soon as you walk through the door, Catherine's hallway walls covered in an eclectic mix of drawings, oil paintings and signage all hung gallery-style. "Hallways can get neglected but they are the first place you see when you come home so should reflect the rest of your home," she says.

The dark walls mean Catherine has had to choose her art carefully. "The art needed to pop against the walls," she says, "so I avoided anything that was too dark. I built the collection over years, sometimes buying art that I liked then finding a place for it, which is not difficult when you have eclectic gallery walls, but I also sourced art for a particular room and wall such as the art in my kitchen – the *This is Where the Magic Happens* poster – as it's very appropriate for a kitchen. I particularly love portraits because you can connect so much more with them."

Catherine's collection has been sourced from many different places. "Antique fairs are my favourite, as you get one offs,' she says. "That's where I bought the picture showing two faces in the dining room – the vendor had all his art lined up on the floor and knew I had to have it as soon as I saw it. It was raining at the time but because it's an original oil painting, it didn't get damaged in the rain."

ABOVE Floating shelves in a corner of the living room contain a varied mix of objects, including one of a series of illustrations from a lookbook in which fashion designer Dries Van Noten collaborated with British illustrator Gill Button.

OPPOSITE The wall behind the sofa, a focal point of the room, has been given over to a gallery wall. Although the walls are dark, colour is introduced into the room through furniture and accessories. Bold hues are found in the art, too, for an atmospheric space that feels anything but gloomy.

She is determined too. Catherine had the artwork in the kitchen painted in China after seeing it online in someone's home. "I couldn't find it anywhere and I knew someone who had a friend in China who was an artist, so I commissioned them to paint it for me."

Catherine has also found her artworks in books. "The small portrait black-and-white prints dotted throughout the flat are illustrations cut out of a 2016 lookbook in which the fashion designer Dries Van Noten collaborated with the illustrator Gill Button," she says. "I love the way the eyes stare at you and the chiselled jaw lines."

PAGE 80 Catherine's hallway is as full of art as the rest of her home, ensuring the apartment's decorative style begins as soon as one enters the home. The portrait of a woman, *Forget Me Not* by Himitsuhana for Mineheart, has been printed onto canvas and placed in a large decorative frame.

PAGE 81 Above a console table in the hallway is a mix of artworks that, although all very different, work well together. The portrait is a giclee print by the artist Rebecca Leigh. The numbers are significant to Catherine and the skull gives them an unexpected twist.

LEFT On the opposite side of the living room is another gallery wall, this one made up almost completely of portraits in mismatched frames. The black-and-white portrait and one on a green background are by Mark Mellon. Top left is *White Dress*, another printed canvas by Himitsuhana for Mineheart. The striking double portrait on the right was bought at an antiques fair.

"I PARTICULARLY LOVE PORTRAITS BECAUSE YOU CAN CONNECT SO MUCH MORE WITH THEM."

BELOW The living room features a wide range of styles, teaming a boho chandelier with a 1970s-style table lamp and a modern sofa alongside a vintage leather armchair. This mix of furnishings allows the art to be equally varied and still sit well together. The large portrait that holds the wall on the left is a print of *Portrait of Madame Mayden* by Amedeo Modigliani.

OPPOSITE In her galley kitchen, Catherine has centred the artwork around a high table and barstools. Three shapely wooden chopping boards hung together (odd numbers always look better) fit the room's function. Catherine saw a similar poster to *This Is Where the Magic Happens* on Instagram and commissioned an artist in China to paint one for her when she could not source the original herself.

LEFT & BELOW This stylish shelfie is mostly monochrome with ceramics adding pops of colour (left). The portrait is another from the collaboration between Dries Van Noten and Gill Button. In the bedroom, a floating corner shelf gives the opportunity for another decorative display above the small bedside table (below).

OPPOSITE A print of *Ribes nigrum*, one of a series of botanical photographs taken by Karl Blossfeldt in the early 20th century, has a wide black frame, which accentuates the details of the image. It was the starting point for this decorative corner, which includes a display of hats and, on a bench, still-life objects. Gold accents tie in with the statement floor lamp.

ART NOTES

How do you choose what to frame?

"I usually frame everything except for art on stretched canvas, but the size of the frame will differ. If I have a small print, I opt for a wider frame and/or a wider mount to lend it some grandeur. I would always get expensive pieces professionally framed with non-reflection UV-protective glass. For cheap prints, I use Ikea frames."

You also mount pictures on wood.

"Yes, the Modigliani behind my sofa is done that way – it's good way to treat a large artwork, as you don't get any glare. If I was o frame it with anti-glare glass, it would be very expensive. Also, it's nice to not have everything framed, as well as a way of preserving a print over time."

What's your one piece of advice on collecting art?

"Go with your heart. If you instantly like a piece, then you will love it forever. And you don't always have to spend a lot of money – you can simply cut pictures out of a book."

MODERN LIFE

June and David Rosenkilde's taste in art is as contemporary as their interior design aesthetic, but their Copenhagen apartment holds a few personal surprises, too.

OPPOSITE In the more relaxed of June and David's two living rooms is a painting by Danish artist Malene Landgreen entitled *Outside Life*. The laid-back mood of the painting fits the feel of the room. Set within the panelling, it offers a modern contrast to the traditional architecture.

For many years, June Rosenkilde thought that buying art was beyond her budget. "As far back as I remember, I went to art galleries and looked at paintings, but could never afford to buy them," she says. "Then, when I was in my twenties and living in Germany, I started work in a print shop. That introduced me to limited-edition prints and the possibility that I could afford to buy original art." Her first purchase was an etching by the German neo-expressionist AR Penck. "It cost me a month's salary, but it was worth it, and that was the start. Art is now so important to me. A home without art is a home without a soul."

Today the etching is one of many artworks found in the light-filled apartment in Copenhagen that June shares with her husband David. Although the building dates from the 19th century, the couple's decor is stylishly modern. The art, too, is mostly contemporary, with inexpensive pieces alongside higher priced ones. She and David buy what they love. "If we fall in love with a piece of art and we can afford it, we buy it and bring it home," says June. "We then look around the house for the perfect spot – we have always managed to find one. We have also found that, once hung, the artwork always feels as though it was meant to be there."

What makes her fall for an artwork? "I see something in it that draws me in, that makes me think about what's in it," she says. "Take the painting in the less formal living room by the Danish artist Malene Landgreen. I love the relaxed posture of the figure – when I look at it, it creates a mindful moment, and that perfectly fits the mood of the room."

Another eye-catching piece is a modern artwork by Michael Kvium that, unusually, spans two walls of an adjoining room. "When I first saw it, it was actually a series of prints that had been framed together," says June. "I really loved it, but it was very long, about 3.5m/11ft 6in. It would have been too long to hang in most private homes, including ours, even though we have large walls." Determined to have it, June wasn't ready to walk away. "So, I asked the artist if he would mind if I split it so it could hang across two walls in this way, and he agreed," she says. "And since then, the artist has divided the artwork into three pieces so that people can hang it as they wish."

Offering quite a different feel is the gallery wall in the kitchen. Here, she and David have combined a wide variety of artworks, from prints and drawings to old family snapshots and professional photographs. "It was so much fun to do," she says. "I framed each piece as I thought it should be framed, with a mix of old and new frames, and then David and I built the wall together. We began with about six pieces and every now and then added another. Now there are about 50 in total. Every single one has a story to tell that is close to our hearts in one way or another. They're also a reminder that art is not something to be afraid of, but something to live with while enjoying life."

RIGHT In the more formal living room, the colour and style of the iconic Le Corbusier leather sofas are picked up in the monochrome artwork. A limited-edition print by Antony Gormley has a black frame that complements the art perfectly. The doors look through to the more colourful dining room.

BELOW Also in this room is an oval-shaped mobile by Malene Landgreen suspended from the ceiling. It is made up of a blue oval shape out of which other shapes have been cut, hence its name *Still Mobile*. The old armchair, with its cracked leather upholstery and feathery seat, is a foil to the smart feel of the room and creates an interesting visual counterpoint.

OPPOSITE Art counterbalances the high ceilings and expansive walls of the apartment. This artwork is made up of three lithographs hung next to each other, across two walls, effectively decorating this corner and adding colour. By Michael Kvium, the triptych is entitled *Where in Hell is God?*.

PAGE 92 While the predominant style of the Rosenkildes' home is contemporary, June has created a vintage corner in the dining room with an old oil painting and much-loved toys. June suspects, but cannot confirm, that the portrait is by the Danish painter Vilhelm Hammershøi, who was known for his subtle, muted colour palette.

"I ASKED THE ARTIST IF HE WOULD MIND IF I SPLIT IT SO IT COULD HANG ACROSS TWO WALLS IN THIS WAY."

LEFT Above an original Bauhaus desk, June has framed three drawings done by a friend. The simplicity of the white frames against the white wall keeps the space feeling light and airy.

BELOW LEFT In June and David's home is a cabinet filled with glassware and ceramics, including these small Baroque porcelain figures that stand on a vintage dish.

BELOW In the dining room, the seating is a mix of mid-century modern chairs, including the Series 7 design by Arne Jacobsen for Fritz Hansen. On the table, alongside a pair of candlesticks stands an antique tea cosy. A collection of vintage candlesticks on a tray decorates the red console.

ART NOTES

Have you ever bought an artwork for a particular space?

"Only once. I really wanted a mobile – something that moves in the air and changes its image before your eyes is enchanting to me. I always knew it would hang in the formal living room because it just felt right."

What's the story behind one of your pieces?

"The portrait of a man playing a guitar was a gift from the family who were my neighbours when I was growing up. Around the age of 14, I was shown into their loft and invited to choose a painting; I chose this one purely because it had an amazing Baroque, gold frame. Some years later, I removed the frame to create a mirror, but I kept the painting. Over time, I came to really appreciate it because it looks like it could have been done by one of my favourite Danish painters, Vilhelm Hammershøi. I've had it checked a couple of times and no one has been able to confirm it, but given the connections of the family who owned it, it could well be. I love its mystery."

How do you display art that can't be hung on a wall?

"In my bedroom are boxes that contain stones and sands that have been collected from countries around the world including Bali, Ecuador and Japan, as well as throughout Europe. Putting them in boxes created an installation that represents our lives. I love that when I wake up, I can lie there and look at them and recall memories of the places we've been."

Your one piece of art advice?

"A good work in a bad frame will never shine 100 per cent, whereas a less good work will be enhanced by the right frame, creating a new and exciting experience."

BELOW In June and David's bedroom, the walls are decorated with boxes that contain stones and sand from countries they have visited. Grouped together in this way, they create an uncommon sculptural display. Above are entomological prints, also collected on their travels.

OPPOSITE On the kitchen gallery wall, treasured pieces include an etching by AR Penck in the bottom right-hand corner. To its left are a photo, *Crazy Horse*, by supermodel and photographer Helena Christensen and a watercolour by animation artist Trylle Vilstrup. Just seen behind the pendant light is a papier-mâché potato by Jörg Immendorff called *Alles was Ihr von mir bekommt.*

FRAMING YOUR ART

PAGES 96-97 From left, a map of London by Kristjana S Williams, *Of Languid Seemed His Mood* by Scarlett Raven, *The Butterfly Man, Vichy* by Sir Peter Blake and *What Now My Love* by Louise Dear have been framed in a variety of styles.

THIS PAGE A mix of frames has been confidently put together to create this bold display. The palette is echoed in the cushions/pillows below.

WHY FRAME?

A frame around an artwork defines its boundaries, setting it apart from the space around it so it can be seen clearly. It is also the finishing touch, comparable to the accessories you add to an outfit, the shoes and jewellery that make a dress or a suit feel complete. It's a similar story with a frame – it gives a finished look that will help show off an artwork at its best.

Conversely, the wrong frame can detract from the art and even overshadow it. It may look unbalanced and can even jar when looking at it. An unsuitable frame can also draw attention away from a piece of art, as you see the frame and not the artwork within it. This doesn't mean you can never use a highly decorative frame, but the image needs to be strong enough that the frame complements it rather than being the star of the show.

How a painting is framed depends on its medium. Oil paintings are not usually framed behind glass as oils pre-date the creation of glass and the tradition of not glazing them continues. It's also because oil paints are robust, but need to be able to breathe. Acrylic paints also need breathability but, being more susceptible to the effects of heat and pollution, are sometimes glazed. Art on paper is always framed behind glass to protect it, as paper is a fragile material, as are watercolour paints and drawing materials.

Frames are often made of wood, which can be stained lighter or darker, painted, gilded or lacquered. Metal frames come in finishes such as silver, gold and bronze, while plastic frames are available in a wide range of colours.

Picture framers can lead you through the process of framing your artwork. They are professionals with years of experience to draw upon and can help edit down both different framing styles as well as the frames themselves. You can also choose from a wide variety of ready-made frames that now go beyond the typical black frames to decorative ones, giving you greater choice to do it yourself. But whichever you choose – and throughout your home you may choose a combination of the two – it's a good idea to understand the principles of framing.

ABOVE Framing a collage of photographs and postcards results in an interesting artwork that helps decorate the corner of a room. A painted frame, simple but vintage in look, ties the collage to the age and style of the cabinet.

Before we get into the details, though, it's useful to know what constitutes framing. There are a variety of different techniques (these are discussed in more detail further on in this chapter) but for much of the time you will be looking at the frame, also called a moulding, which is the solid structure, usually made of wood, metal or plastic, that goes round your artwork. Then there is the mount/mat (also called a passe-partout), which is the card that surrounds the picture within the frame or on which the image sits within the frame. The best quality is conservation-grade mount/mat, which will not degrade and turn yellow over time.

MATCHING A FRAME TO AN ARTWORK

Some artists, especially when it comes to original art, will create an artwork with an idea of the frame they want around it. You should be able to discuss this with the artist, or someone from the gallery you are buying the artwork from, and this gives you a useful starting point.

If you're starting from scratch, the first thing to do is consider the style of painting. If it is an oil painting, whether recently painted or vintage, in a more classical style, then a traditional-style frame, such as a gilt or carved wooden frame, will complement the artwork. An abstract print will suit a more streamlined, less ornate frame.

With oil paintings, the width of the moulding is important as this can vary hugely – visit any art gallery and you will see that the frames of oil paintings come in a wide variety of sizes. With large paintings, the width of the moulding needs to be in scale with the image – too small and it will feel squeezed. With smaller paintings, though, you can go extra-wide if you like – this will make the artwork appear larger and more impactful, while at the same time leading your eye to the image itself.

The other major consideration is the colours found in the artwork. There is a temptation to take the decor of your room into account but there is no need. In choosing the artwork, you've already decided whether you want it to complement or contrast the room's decor, so now you just need to make sure the frame and image work as one in your room.

Choose a frame in a colour or tone that you find in the artwork and you will find that the two go together well. If you pick a frame in contrasting colour, there's a risk it will dominate. Take a black-and-white photograph for instance; put it in a bright red frame, and the first thing you will see

when looking at it is the frame, not the photograph. However, frame the photograph in a slim black frame and your eye will go straight to the image.

Be careful with black frames, though. They are popular, and often inexpensive, but black is a heavy colour and can dominate an artwork. In a gallery wall, a mass of thick black frames can make it difficult for you to focus on the artworks. As a rule of thumb, choose a black frame if the image within it has black or dark colours, as this anchors the artwork to the frame.

When choosing a mount/mat, the simplest option is a shade of white that matches the colour of the paper the artwork is on. You may, of course, choose a coloured mount/mat, but this can impose on the artwork. In this case, you may want to consider a double mount/mat (see Framing Styles on page 109).

OPPOSITE LEFT The medieval-style painting of the Virgin Mary and Jesus with its rich gold tones fits the highly ornate gilt frame, ensuring it takes pride of place above the antique chest of drawers.

OPPOSITE RIGHT As well as the colours within a painting, a frame can be used to tie an artwork to the rest of the room. In this bedroom, although the print is in black and white, the shade of the frame links it to the shelf and wall light.

ABOVE LEFT A print of the iconic painting *Chinese Girl* by Vladimir Tretchikoff has been placed in an elegant vintage frame that echoes its colours.

ABOVE RIGHT In this corner, the larger photograph has been framed with a standard white mount/mat and simple black frame, while the much smaller image has been finished with a wide mount and frame. The difference in scale draws the eye and creates an interesting contrast.

LEFT Canvas frames have been propped against one another with mostly black-and-white pictures stuck into corners instead of filling the space. This unusual collage is accessorized with books and decorative objects in a similar palette of colours and materials.

PROTECTING ART

Glazing your artwork sounds like a straightforward process, but there are several options available here too.

The least expensive choice is acrylic (also known as Perspex or Plexiglass), a type of plastic that will protect a painting against moisture and pollution but does not have the clarity of glass. Standard glass has better clarity than acrylic, but will show reflections that can be distracting. Non-reflective glass is the next step up, as it does have some anti-reflective properties, but it can make the image appear blurry when viewed close up.

None of these options offer protection against ultra-violet (UV) rays from sunlight, which can fade artworks on paper and photographs over time. For that, you will need the more expensive anti-reflective glass that comes with UV protection. There are three levels: AR70 screens out 70 per cent of harmful UV rays, AR92 screens out 92 percent and AR99 screens outs 99 per cent of UV rays. This last one is also called museum glass, because it is designed for use in museum and gallery settings, and is the highest quality available.

The other enemy of art is moisture, and if you're wanting to display art in rooms that have a high moisture content, such as a bathroom, make sure the artwork is completely sealed. You can use aluminium foil sealing tape yourself, but if you have an artwork that is valuable, either personally or financially, then it is best to take it to a professional framer and explain that the artwork will be hung in a bathroom. Remember, though, this will not stop the glass from fogging up, as a mirror does when you have a hot shower.

LEFT A collection of abstracts has a striking effect in this bedroom. Each frame has been chosen to suit the style of the work within it, ensuring that the focus is on the art. A striped throw echoes the graphic patterns and the round mirror breaks up the straight lines.

OPPOSITE Dark walls can make any artwork stand out. In this living room, the off-white frame around the print, *Black With Many White Swirls* by Briggs Edward Solomon from ArtStar, has a simplicity that allows the bold, abstract artwork to shine.

OPPOSITE The frame of this artwork blends into the picture, focusing attention on the emotive image that draws the viewer in. The colours of the artwork are found in the collection of vases below – a few have been turned on their side, tops facing outward, for visual variety.

LEFT A vintage gilt frame is an unexpected but inspired choice for this monochrome print. The worn sections tone down the gold, however, so the contrast isn't so great that it jars.

ABOVE An oil painting in the dining room of Daniel Heckscher's home – by his grandfather, a talented amateur artist – complements the colours of the space and is also a constant reminder of a loved one.

RIGHT A three-dimensional artwork in a rich shade of orange-red is left unframed, emphasizing the difference between it and the panelled wall on which it hangs. The colour combination of chairs and cushions/pillows, however, helps integrate the art into the space.

LEFT This gallery wall features a range of unconnected images in a variety of frames, but the beautifully coloured wallpaper behind them creates a link between them all for a display that is eclectic and eye-catching.

ABOVE Tongue-in-cheek artworks – mug shots of Jane Fonda and Frank Sinatra, scaled up and re-coloured by the artist Russell Young for his series of *Pig Portraits* – fit the casual mood of the living room.

PAGE 112 Above doors and doorways are favourite places for art in Sarah and Ned's home. In the study, over the doorway leading into the hall, is an oil painting by Ned's mother, artist Kate Corbett-Winder. The blues contrast with the mustard walls but are found elsewhere in the room's furniture and accessories.

PAGE 113 In the same room, the opposite wall between two windows is dominated by a large photographic print, *Eden-Roc Pool* by Slim Aarons. Although it is different in style to the painting, the colours of the two works are similar enough that they can sit together in the same room.

OPPOSITE In the kitchen, Sarah replaced one large painting with a gallery wall that works better in the space and brings character with a mix of round and rectangular pieces. The

largest work is *Apollo and Daphne II* by Glyn Morgan. To the right are a blue painting by Sarah, with her son's shoe resting on top of the frame, and one of a pair of limited-edition prints by Claudia Valsells. On either side of the candle sconce on the bottom row are *Scores on the Door* by Def Trax and *Oven Glove* by Hugo Guinness.

ABOVE The kitchen is a fabulously decorative space with all sorts of objects on display. On the ledge is the other of Claudia Valsells' prints. Above it is *Corkscrew* by Hugo Guinness. A piece of art created by Ned is paired with a beautifully ornate frame.

RIGHT A ledge made from a piece of leftover cornicing in the bar area of the kitchen is a shelf that holds a painting by Kate Corbett-Winder and art by her grandchildren.

LEFT & BELOW In the spare room, blue and white hand-painted stripes by artist Lucy Mahon cover the walls and ceiling, creating art directly on the walls (left). The stripes are a backdrop to four framed skeleton coral prints beside the headboard and, in a contrast to the blue of the room, a pair of striking monochrome prints on the longer wall (below).

ABOVE Within mouldings and on a narrow ledge, the stairwell from the first to the top floor contains a gallery wall that is forever changing, with art and even some of Sarah's collection of handbags going on display.

OPPOSITE Sarah and Ned's ensuite bathroom has a luxurious feel, with the Burlington bathtub and richly textured fabrics. Between the decorative wall lights hangs an evocative print of the Italian coastal village of Portofino by Slim Aarons. It has been printed on a sheet of Perspex/Plexiglass, which is more moisture resistant than paper.

"NED'S MOTHER IS AN ARTIST, SO SHE GIVES US PAINTINGS, AND WE LIKE TO FRAME THE CHILDREN'S ART – THAT INNOCENCE IS HARD TO ACHIEVE AS AN ADULT."

ABOVE Sarah and Ned's daughter's room teams pink stripes with florals for a maximalist vibe. Artwork covers the walls and largely follows the floral theme. Although not particularly child-orientated, it still suits the room. The print above the bed by Emerald Blenkin complements the floral artworks on the left.

OPPOSITE This child's room has subtle green walls but is lifted by colourful accessories. The alphabet wall hanging by Moppet covers much of the wall, adding texture and colour but also a dose of fun. It is teamed with a pink-framed mirror and a postcard elevated to art with a gilt frame.

LEFT & BELOW Sarah and Ned's bedroom at the top of the house is also a riot of stripes, this time in a vibrant orange (left). The room's sloping wall doesn't allow for art behind the bed, but works by Kate Corbett-Winder are hung to the left of the window and in the adjacent hallway. The artwork of three animal skulls in a distressed frame was created by Ned (below).

OPPOSITE The colour theme of the children's bathroom is red with accessories including all the artworks featuring the colour against the red and cream striped wallpaper. Splatterware plates add a different shape and visual interest to one wall.

ART NOTES

Have you a favourite artwork?

"A pair of paintings by the Spanish artist Claudia Valsells, who is known for her work in colour – they're earthy and have a strength to them, which works perfectly with the palette of our home. I also love the simplicity and size of the paintings. They are supposed to sit together, but I have separated them to be on either side of the kitchen. They bring me a lot of joy."

How do you do artwork on wallpaper?

"They both need to really complement each other so the colours work together or the artwork has to be such a contrast that the boldness makes it work."

What's your one piece of advice on collecting art?

"Be honest with yourself. Will the artwork go with your existing family of art and does it suit the space where it is going to live? I love lots of art, but I appreciate that it won't always work in our house. As much as I am an impulsive art buyer, I always make sure that any new piece will be a great addition to the family!"

HOW TO HANG
YOUR ART

Where should you hang your art? The answer is anywhere you wish. Every wall of your home is a blank canvas that can be filled with paintings, prints and photography. But before you merrily begin hammering hooks into walls, it's best to make a plan so you don't do anything you might regret later.

Start by considering the space as a whole. Is there a wall or walls that would suit a larger statement piece of art? Where could you create a gallery wall? Is there a small or forgotten space that could be made more interesting by hanging an artwork there?

All this may sound daunting, but you can make it easier by first thinking about the room's focal point, the spot your eye is naturally drawn to when you walk in. In a room with a mantelpiece, for instance, this will be the wall above it. Large pieces of furniture can also help give you a focal point – in a living room, it could be the wall above the sofa; in a bedroom, it's the wall above the headboard. A focal point gives you a centre from which to start.

In a large, open-plan living space, you may have multiple options. In this case, start by zoning the different areas – living, dining and office, for example – and then decide which wall or feature will be the focal point for each. Along with the furnishings, the style of art you choose will help define the area's function. If your room doesn't have an obvious focal point such as a mantelpiece, opt for the largest empty wall. Hanging art there will draw the eye and allow you to design the rest of the room around it.

Once you have decided on your main focal point, look around the room and decide where else you can hang art, for example on the wall opposite the mantel. Other possibilities include the narrow section of wall between windows, above a console or sideboard/credenza and behind a door.

But, a word of warning: you need a maintain a hierarchy in the artworks so when you walk into a room, your eye naturally falls to your focal point before travelling round the room in a way that feels comfortable. If the artworks fight each other for attention, the room will feel unbalanced.

PAGES 122–123 In the entrance to his home, artist Fred Ingrams has hung four of his oil paintings in hues of blue, yellow and green. There is a symmetry in the choice of frames. Smaller artworks propped on the table add extra interest.

OPPOSITE The predominantly grey palette of the William Gear print fits the colour scheme of this dining area, with the yellow and blue adding pops of warming colour. Within an open-plan space, art can give each zone its own character.

ABOVE The red of the headboard is picked up in only some of the art in this bedroom, but taken as a whole, the gallery wall complements the bed, which is the room's statement piece of furniture.

For example, the artwork above your sofa can be larger than the one above the mantelpiece, as long as its style and colour palette do not overshadow the focal piece. An example of this is the living room in Sandra Barrio von Hurter's living room on pages 30–31 – the painting above the sofa may be large, but the colours are more muted, allowing the white of the framed headdress above the mantelpiece to sing out loudly.

HOW TO HANG

What is the correct height at which to hang art? In most cases, you should hang your artwork so the middle of the piece is at eye level. This is the case even if you have high ceilings; don't be tempted to hang your art too far up the wall, as you don't want to be looking up at them. There are some exceptions to this, though. With a gallery wall, images can go above or below your eyeline. You can also hang art in a way that draws your eye into unexpected places, such as placing two or three artworks in a staggered formation on one side of a sofa or bed so the lowest one sits partially or even completely parallel to the furniture.

Groups of paintings can be hung to one side but a single piece of artwork, especially a large one, will always look best dead centre. For artwork above furniture, whether it be a sofa or table, up to about 30cm/12in above the top of the furniture is about right. Anything under a 10cm/4in gap will feel cramped, so if your wall doesn't have the height to allow this gap, it's better to prop it instead (for more guidance on propping, see page 139).

With art above a sofa, especially one that is low-slung, it's also worth doing a seat test. Sit down and lean your head back; if you collide with the bottom of the painting, then it needs to go higher.

LINE OF SIGHT

Sight lines are a key concept in interior design and you can use them to hang your art in ways that make your home look and feel balanced and cohesive.

What are sight lines? Put simply, they are the view of one room that you have from another, and when decorating, whether with paint or art, keeping this idea in mind will help you harmoniously link the rooms together.

For instance, use green on the walls in a hallway and a clashing yellow in the adjoining living room and you may find that both spaces end up feeling discordant, as if they belong in different homes. This is because the sight lines of the rooms – looking into the living room from the hallway and vice versa – show the jarring colour clash.

When applying this to art, you need to make sure the art you see in one room fits with the art you can see in the next.

OPPOSITE LEFT A corner of a room is made interesting with a print of Sir Howard Hodgkin's *Green Room* – the red of the painting is also found in the side table. Together they make a contemporary contrast to the traditional-style chair.

OPPOSITE RIGHT Postcards and photographs attached with pegs/clothespins to a length of string create a renter-friendly art display above the bed, and one that be easily and quickly changed, too.

ABOVE LEFT Variations on a theme come together for a chic look. The bold triangular shape in the print is in conversation with the leaf in the vase and with the traditional motif carved into the mantelpiece.

ABOVE RIGHT A trio of artworks, including the print *Geometric* by Jesus Perea (below left), predominantly in black, add sophistication to pale pink walls. The configuration takes into account the brass wall lamp and incorporates it into the arrangement.

So, if you have a gallery wall that's busy with lots of smaller pieces of art in your hallway which can be seen from your living room, it would be best to select a few larger works for this room to temper the look; seeing two busy walls is likely to feel like visual overload.

Sight lines are also used to give rooms a sense of connection. Again, thinking of paint colours, if a living room is in a soft blue, having that same shade in the dining room next door creates a cohesive feel. One way to introduce the colour is with art – hang an artwork featuring the shade of blue in the dining room and in a place where it can be seen from the living room, and the eye will be led from one room to the next.

A SENSE OF SCALE

A statement piece of artwork needs to hold the room and look like it belongs in the space – size and scale play a big part in achieving this.

Choose an artwork that is too small for the wall, and it will look and feel lost – it needs to fill at least 50 per cent of the space. At the same time, you need to give the artwork space to breathe; one that fills almost all the wall, with just a narrow border around it, will appear hemmed in and make the room feel claustrophobic.

OPPOSITE A framed line drawing adds an understated, contemporary touch to a panelled bedroom. In the hallway, the reds and yellows of the artworks can be found in the living room beyond.

ABOVE RIGHT The pink of the wall is reflected in the colours of a large abstract by Karl Troels Sandegård. On the floor, two works by Morten Ernlund Jørgensen add a shot of contrasting sharper colour. Propped against the wall, they feel more relaxed.

RIGHT What would otherwise be a neglected corner of this room is given personality with the addition of art. The palette works with the strong colour of the walls, but also picks up the shades of yellow found in the room beyond, linking the two spaces. Below the art, a vintage wooden chair with a stack of books resembles a still life.

Bijou artworks can work beyond the gallery wall but you need to make sure that they, too, don't get lost. Hang them above a console table, a chest of drawers/dresser or a single chair – the furniture gives the set-up scale, making the artwork fit the space and drawing the eye towards it.

Small pieces are also perfect for giving often forgotten or awkward corners a stylistic lift, bringing these spaces into the room and making it feel decoratively complete. Hanging a print or painting behind a door creates a lovely surprise when the door is closed, for example. Just don't hang it too high, but at a level where you can easily see it. And as small pieces need to be appreciated close up, don't place a piece of furniture in front of the artwork so you can't get close to it.

COLOUR & PATTERN

Do you treat artworks differently when hanging them on a richly coloured wall? In terms of the art itself, you don't need to be concerned about limiting your selection to artworks that include the same colour as the background.

ABOVE Monochrome botanical prints, framed in black and hung in a grid formation, create an elegant display that perfectly matches the style of this living room. They add decoration without dominating the room.

RIGHT A series of black-and-white photographs hung horizontally across the living room wall makes a cool style statement as well as decorating a vast stretch of wall with a small number of pieces.

Instead of being centred above the sofa, this signed lithograph by Enric Cormenzana is hung at one end. To balance this placement, two smaller pictures in a similar colour palette are placed at a lower angle and anchored by the side table.

At a Royal Academy of Arts Summer Exhibition in London, coordinated by artist Grayson Perry, the walls of one room were painted a bright, sunshine yellow, yet this enhanced, rather than detracted from the artworks hung on the wall, despite them being in a wide range of styles and colours. However, it's best not to throw a variety of decorative frames into the mix; keep them more low-key.

Art hung on a wallpapered background can be impressive and add an element of fun, too. It is an eclectic look, though, so if that's not what you're after, then it's best avoided. If you do want to give it a go, make sure the artwork stands out – you don't want it to blend into the wallpaper. If you want to really up the ante, add a decorative frame, too.

LEFT On a focal wall, patterned wallpaper and a gallery of artwork create an impactful display. The art, including a portrait of a woman by Zoë Pawlak, picks out the blue on the sofa, and matching frames colour ensure a unified look.

ABOVE A figurative vintage painting is very different to the bold wallpaper behind it, ensuring the art stands out. However, the pink of the flowers in the painting picks up on the similar tones in the wallpaper and the chairs.

OPPOSITE On an upper staircase that only the family sees is a "good times" gallery wall that includes a mix of photographs and family mementoes. The use of frames and mounts/mats in a similar style keeps it all cohesive.

RIGHT This staircase gallery wall is a celebration of black culture. It features Eliza Southwood's iconic poster *London is the Place for Me*, which depicts the arrival of the *Empire Windrush* from Jamaica in 1948, and a print by Curly and the Cloud. The dark paint colour below the dado/chair rail helps all the vibrant colours to sing out.

ABOVE A pair of moodboard-style displays propped up on chest of drawers creates a miniature gallery wall in this studio and adds a sense of fun to the space, accentuated by the oversized wall clock above.

THE GALLERY WALL

One of the most popular art displays, this is certainly an eye-catching way of adding visual interest to a room. There are a variety of methods for making a gallery wall: the art can follow a look and theme, or the collection can be eclectic, featuring a mix of styles. You can choose a relaxed and flowing formation or a grid for a tidier look.

Using the same style and colour of frame throughout is a way of tying the collection together. However, if the artworks are very different both in style and medium, then a mix of frames in a variety of colours will give a wall a sense of depth.

Gallery walls don't have to be just art, though. Some of the most arresting and successful gallery walls are, in fact, memory walls – a combination of art and memorabilia that tell the story of you and your family. So alongside photographs and artworks that capture holiday memories and special moments, you could display a poster of a favourite exhibition, tickets to a once-in-a-lifetime concert and a framed piece of clothing that means something to you.

ASK AN EXPERT:
How to hang a gallery wall

Creating a gallery wall doesn't have to be daunting. Sim Takhar of The Old Bank Vault gallery explains.

1 "When working with a horizontal area, I always start on the left-hand side – that is the way most of us read, so it feels logical. Your first artwork should be about one-third of the way in."

2 "Never start on the wall. Instead, take the measurements of the wall and then recreate the space on the floor directly in front of it, even if you need to move furniture out of the way. This helps you visualize how everything will look on the wall."

3 "Take the artwork that stands out the most, and then place it in the left-hand position it would be on the wall, but on the floor. Then look at the other pieces you want to include, thinking about size and colour. The aim is to bring together all the pieces so they feel like one large artwork."

4 "When positioning them above or below each other, make sure they overlap each other by at least a quarter; anything less and it looks as though you tried to line them up but got it wrong."

5 "The gaps between each artwork do not need to be the same – some might look better with more space to breathe, while others work best in a cluster. I start with either a combination of 3cm/1¼in and 6cm/2½in or 4cm/1½in and 8cm/3in gaps between pieces, and then adjust from there."

6 "Move the artworks around until they look and feel cohesive; it's a bit like doing a puzzle! With a horizontal wall, I like to keep the art on a central line and a little above or below it."

7 "Once you're happy with the look, you're ready to hang. Treat the floor arrangement as a loose sketch – you don't need to be precise to the millimetre – but make sure you hang straight."

8 "To hang, again begin on the left and work your way across. Hang your first artwork at your eyeline. Each time you hang a piece, stand back and look before you hang the next one."

9 "If doing a vertical wall, start in the middle and then go up and down. Don't be afraid to go as low or as high as you like."

10 "When doing a stairwell, recreate the ascending shape on the floor by placing masking tape or string at a 45-degree angle, using that as your baseline when placing your art."

RIGHT The dark colour of the walls makes the black-and-white prints stand out. The eclectic mix fits the quirky feel of this cottage and its combination of vintage furniture and accessories.

OPPOSITE This monochrome gallery wall is a mix of prints, drawings and photographs with decorative plates breaking up the straight lines and adding an extra decorative touch.

BELOW Photos in a wide variety of sizes, some in black-and-white and others in full colour, and all framed in black, have been carefully hung to cover almost the entire wall from top to bottom.

PROPPING

Art doesn't just have to be hung on walls. In fact, it can look great propped on a flat surface whether it be a sideboard/credenza, dressing table, shelf, bedside table or even the floor.

Propping an artwork creates a more relaxed vibe, so it's suited to rooms or areas where you want a laid-back mood to prevail. Propping also allows you to mix art with other objects such as ornaments and books to create vignettes that make a room interesting.

When propping larger pieces on furniture, think about scale. There needs to be a sense of balance between the art and the furniture – an enormous picture on a small table will look odd and feel disconcerting.

You can also prop artworks of staggered sizes against each other so that they overlap slightly. With this set-up, it's not so much about each individual artwork but that together they create a whole statement piece. However, do make sure the pieces are linked in some way, whether that be through the artworks themselves (their colour and style) or their frames.

Shelves are excellent places to showcase smaller artworks. You can mix them in with other pieces – in the kitchen, prop them between cups, bowls and potted plants or, in the living room, between candlesticks and books. You can even give over an entire shelf to them, varying the sizes and shapes, but as before, ensuring there is something that links them.

Propped on the floor, artworks can make a real impact but only if the rest of the space is fairly sparse. If not, they will look as though they just haven't been put away. They look particularly good against wooden floors.

OPPOSITE A double shelf propped with artworks make a real style statement in this living room. The layered feel of the shelves suits the boho style of the room with its long sofa, which has been made cosy with sheepskin rugs and cushions/pillows.

ABOVE In this variation on a gallery wall, boxed shelves take up one wall and disguise stairs to a platform bedroom. They are filled with a variety of objects, providing ample storage as well as decoration.

LEFT Images stuck on the wall with tape are balanced by the single framed print to the right. The palette, based on the dark blue of the walls, has been kept simple and an extra decorative flourish is provided by the propped oars.

OPPOSITE Patterned monochrome wallpaper creates a visually arresting backdrop to a gallery wall of family photos. The frames and mounts/mats are in a palette of just a few colours, which helps unify the look so that the wall doesn't appear too busy.

UP CLOSE & PERSONAL

Photographs of family and friends add a personal touch to your home and prompt memories of people you love, and happy times spent together. They can, though, be tricky to display in a way that does not jar with the art – and decor – of the rest of your home.

One way that does work is combining your personal images with others, whether they be photographs or art, so your family photos become part of your entire collection. When displaying them on a wall, go boho with a mix of mounts and frames. Conversely, white frames and mounts tie in both colour and black-and-white images super stylishly.

Printing photographs in black and white makes them instantly look chic and more professional, especially if you use mounts/mats and the same style frame. A grid formation on a wall complements this style well, but it looks equally strong on a shelf.

On shelves, follow the tips on propping (see page 139): make sure some overlap the other – smaller ones do this well – and if you love an eclectic look, add in ornaments and houseplants.If you like the idea of a statement photograph, a landscape with family or friends pictured within the setting looks more sophisticated than a close-up.

LET THERE BE LIGHT

Picture lights are a traditional way of highlighting art, but you don't need them to enjoy the paintings and prints on your walls. If you like the effect they give and want to highlight your art using them, it is best to install them quite close to the artwork, about 5–7cm/2–2¾in above it. Do also stand back from the wall to make sure the light isn't obscuring the artwork.

You can also use ceiling-mounted spotlights; these need to be set at a 30-degree angle so that the light beam hits the centre of the artwork. This way you avoid casting shadows over it, and also reduce reflective glare.

Track lights can work in a similar way and are, of course, easier to install, but they best suit a contemporary home. You can also use table and floor lamps to subtly highlight an artwork, placing the lamp so the light hits the mid-point.

The enemy of art is ultra-violet (UV) light that, over time, will fade paintings, especially those on paper, and photographs. To prevent this, keep your art out of direct sunlight. If it is displayed in a south-facing room that receives a lot of bright light, consider investing in art glass that screens out UV rays and helps with glare. For artificial lighting, use LED bulbs that emit no UV and little heat.

ASK AN EXPERT:
Mixing old and new

Michelle Adams of online marketplace Artfully Walls explains how to use art to juxtapose the traditional with the contemporary to create a visually stimulating space.

Once, different design styles stayed resolutely separate. A beautiful dress was worn with high heels, a historic house was filled with antique furniture and a modern apartment with sleek stainless steel. But over the past couple of decades, mixing design styles has become an accepted – and highly sought-after – concept in design. So today, a dress is often teamed with trainers and polished marble floors and gleaming brass fixtures combined with neon signage and modern art.

The end result of this mixing of styles is called "stylistic tension", the term describing the energy and visual excitement that is created by juxtaposing contrasts. "This same idea can be applied to how you introduce art in the home," says Michelle Adams, the founder of online art store Artfully Walls. "It will help your home feel layered, storied and collected over time."

How does it work? "An overly formal living room can instantly feel more modern and relaxed by introducing edgy or contemporary art," says Michelle. "Conversely, modern decor can be made to feel warmer and more timeless by adding vintage oil paintings." To apply this idea to your home, look around and identify areas that feel a bit dull or flat. "Then, take note of its current style," advises Michelle. "Is it traditional, contemporary, country, urban, trendy, minimalist or maximalist? Then select a piece of decor or artwork that represents the exact opposite style. For example, you could hang a modern abstract work in a streamlined frame above a historic traditional mantel, or place an oil painting of a landscape or still life in an ornate gilded frame in a bedroom that's sleek and modern." You can do this in every room of your home. "If you have a fancy dining room with a stately china cabinet and traditional chairs, try introducing bright and beautiful floral pieces or interesting abstracts."

Stylistic tension can also make a modern space feel more sophisticated and polished by the addition of traditional art. "In fact," says Michelle, "one of my favourite combinations is Ikea's white lacquered cabinetry with ornate gold frames and antique oil paintings, which you can find at flea markets or online."

ABOVE A contemporary artwork by Liza Giles provides a contrasting modern touch to the shabby chic decor of this living room, without disrupting the neutral colour palette. It doesn't jar, but adds an interesting visual twist.

RIGHT An old painting in a large, ornate frame is the main event in this corner of a living room. Its traditional style is complemented by an antique console and candlestick, but the modern lamp base and drum shade bring it up to date for a look that suits a modern home.

The bright, modern stripes of Bridget Riley's *Rose Rose* print present quite the contrast to the rustic aesthetic of the rest of the room. The colours give the space a lift for a mood that is fun and cheerful.

THREE DIFFERENT LOOKS

ABOVE LEFT A large floral print is the starting point of this arrangement with the artworks and frames around it echoing the tones found within it. The black-and-white cloud print is a monochrome foil to the pink. The table lamp matches the scale of the floral print, while the woven animal head is unexpected and eye-catching.

ABOVE RIGHT Three very different, but equally peaceful, images create a relaxed mood, which is enhanced by the white table lamp with its soft lines. The juxtaposition of the decorative candelabra with pared-back artworks creates a visually more interesting display.

LEFT Just two artworks propped on the table create this arresting scene, the bright colours complementing each other and the sizes in scale for balance. The curved lines of the table lamp and the woven basket below reflect the curves in the smaller image and complete the look.

All art from Artfully Walls.

HANGING AN ARTWORK

1 Hold your artwork up to the wall to find the right place. Use a spirit level to make sure it is perfectly straight.

2 When you are happy with the position, use a pencil to very lightly mark a dot on the wall at the centre of the top of the frame.

3 Holding the artwork, pull the wire or cord attached to hang it upwards evenly from the centre so it is taut and forms an apex. Use a measuring tape to measure the distance from this apex to the top of the artwork frame. This length is called the drop.

4 The drop is the length the picture hook should be from the central point you marked on the wall. Measure the drop straight down from this mark – this is where the hook should be fixed into the wall.

Depending on the wall and size of the piece, the hooks and method will be different (see the options listed on the right).

BELOW The homeowner painted these two artworks in his favourite colours because he couldn't find exactly what he wanted. Contemporary in style, they are part of the room's stylish mix of modern and vintage pieces.

TOOLS YOU WILL NEED

Hammer: *For hammering nails into walls*

Spirit level: *Place this across the top of your artwork when placing it against the wall to ensure it is straight.*

Measuring tape: *Use to measure the drop and the distance between pictures when creating a gallery wall. You can also use a ruler for smaller spaces.*

Pencil: *A soft lead pencil for lightly marking the wall.*

Picture hook with pins: *For dry walls and partition walls, use a metal hook with either two or three nails (depending on the size of your artwork). These are available for weights of 4.5–45kg/10–100lb. For a large artwork, use two hooks, with each one placed at a third of the width of the frame.*

Plastic picture hook: *These acrylic hooks with small metal pins are designed for hard plaster walls. Best for light- to mediumweight artworks.*

Multi-position picture hook: *An acrylic picture hook with pins, as above, but with multiple small hooks. For lightweight artworks.*

Rawlplug/anchor and screw: *For external walls/hard brick. While plastic picture hooks are designed for such walls, the safest method when hanging pictures on hard walls is to drill into the wall and insert a screw into a rawlplug/anchor.*

Steel claw drywall picture hanger: *For drywall or plasterboard walls. Simply push the hooks into the wall to lock them in. Available to hold weights of 7–30kg/15–66lb.*

Split batten: *To carry heavy pictures and mirrors on all walls. One half of the batten is fixed to the frame of the artwork. Another batten of the same length is then fixed to the wall with a rawlplug/anchor and screws. The batten on the frame slots onto the one on the wall.*

J-rail system: *A horizontal track that is fixed to the wall with screws and with a j-shaped hook attached. Other attachments are attached to steel cords that hang down. For rentals, if you are permitted limited drilling into a wall, and for walls protected by conservation orders.*

Command™ Strips: *With no need for nails, these strips can be used on smooth surfaces including walls, tiles, glass and wood and come off cleanly, so are ideal for rental homes. Best suited to lightweight artworks.*

SELF REFLECTION

The art in Natalie Lee's home is big
on colour, emotion and diversity.

OPPOSITE The painted brick wall of
Natalie's kitchen extension is decorated with
a large banner made by Alice Gabb, the size
of it making no other decoration necessary.
Natalie loved the words and commissioned
the velvet banner in the colour of her choice.
Below it, the throw and cushions/pillows
complement the hues of the banner.

Natalie Lee's favourite artwork is a banner that transforms
a blank white wall in her kitchen into an eye-catching space.
It features the words "No one belongs here more than you",
handwritten onto vintage velvet fabric and finished with
fringing. "I saw it and really loved the phrase," says Natalie.
"Growing up mixed race, there was always an issue with
identity, not really knowing where I fitted in. But now, after
talking about it and writing my book, a memoir called *Feeling
Myself*, I am more comfortable with who I am. This banner
is perfect for me. It fills up my soul whenever I see it."

Natalie doesn't shy away from expressing her personality
in her home, and art is key to her creating a space that
reflects who she is. It pops up everywhere, not just hung on
walls but propped on mantelpieces, floors, shelves, and even
the headboard of her bed. "I buy what I love, pieces that are
colourful and fun, and I put them wherever there is room,"
she says. "At the same time, there is a lack of representation
in the art world so I also make sure black and brown people
feature among the pieces that I own."

A particularly striking artwork in the living room is a
portrait of a young black woman called *Let Go of Your Past*.
Rich in pattern and colour, the limited-edition print features
a vibrant shade of green that inspired Natalie to drench the
room in the same hue. "It's by Caroline Chinakwe – I love
how she uses colour," says Natalie.

While this artwork holds an entire wall on its own, in
the kitchen Natalie has filled the walls with numerous pieces
of art. Above the work surface is a long shelf on which sit
colourful prints in different shapes and sizes. "A kitchen can
be boring, so I wanted to create a focal point with art," says
Natalie. In the adjoining kitchen extension, as well as the
velver banner, a number of prints cleverly frame a vintage
sideboard/credenza with some hung low alongside it and
others above. The mix of art here includes posters bought
from a typography exhibition and colourful prints, the
combination set off by industrial-style wall lights and made
lush with an abundance of houseplants. "This area is where
I spend most of my time," she says.

A narrow wall to the right is made interesting by two
portraits hung vertically. The top one is of Nina Simone;
the one below is of Natalie and was painted by artist
Nelly Randall as part of a series of paintings of women she
considered important advocates for body positivity. It's not
the only time Natalie has been a muse, however. Josie Levine,
whose work explores the female form, created a beautiful
line drawing of her and artist Louise Dear painted a large
colourful portrait of Natalie. "It was a life-affirming moment
when I discovered that I had inspired Louise to paint me," she
says. "I absolutely love the work, but it felt a bit narcissistic to
have more pictures of me at home, so I gave it to my mum!"

ABOVE In the entrance hallway, the stairs, painted orange, announce the personality and spirit of Natalie's home. Works by artists of diverse heritage hang on the wall.

RIGHT On the opposite wall in the kitchen extension, artworks are ranged around a vintage sideboard/credenza. Between the wall lights is *Colonial Beauty Elephant* by Johnathan Reiner and to the right are posters by graphic artist Anthony Burrill bought from a typography exhibition. On the narrow wall, a print of *Nina Simone* by Tim Fowler hangs above an original portrait of Natalie by Nelly Randall.

In the kitchen, a long shelf allows space for art and adds interest to what would otherwise be a blank wall. Propped and overlapping, the display fits the more relaxed mood of this room. Closest to this side is *Rainbow* by Rose Stallard and at the far end is a work by Marylou Faure. On the work surface is a painting of Natalie's torso by Nelly Randall.

ABOVE Natalie was drawn to the thought behind the words of this limited-edition print, *Facing the Tiger* by Fei Alexeli from The Old Bank Vault. It inspired a big cat theme for the mantelpiece, where it is flanked by two leopard candlesticks.

RIGHT Natalie has created a bar on an old butcher's trolley. It is given a pop of colour by a *Magnifique* typographic poster from Gayle Mansfield Designs, which tones with the pale pink wall behind.

OPPOSITE The statement piece of art in the living room is a bold limited-edition print called *Let Go Of Your Past* by Caroline Chinakwe. The wall colour is the same shade of green as in the print – Natalie was inspired by it when she decided to repaint the room.

RIGHT A pair of gilt-framed mirrors adorns the mantelpiece. Their ornate style is a perfect fit for the room, but at the same time they do not overshadow the print opposite, which is seen here reflected in the glass.

"I BUY WHAT I LOVE, PIECES THAT ARE COLOURFUL AND FUN, AND I PUT THEM WHEREVER THERE IS ROOM."

LEFT Natalie's home is full of colour, from the orange staircase to the living room colour-drenched in green and the next room in shades of pink. Her art collection is equally vibrant and full of character.

ABOVE In Natalie's bedroom, the figurative artwork on the mantelpiece takes centre stage. On the mantelpiece and around the hearth of the disused fireplace is a mix of vintage and contemporary art.

ABOVE RIGHT A brick painted with an eye motif is a cool DIY artwork.

OPPOSITE A bold stripe behind the bed sets the tone of the room with its colourful cushions/pillows and accessories. The three prints, in a similar style and colour, were bought online. Natalie placed them in matching pink frames before propping them on the headboard, an easy way to display art.

ART NOTES

Is there an artwork that reflects the themes of your book?
"The artwork on the mantelpiece in my bedroom. It shows a topless woman being unapologetically feminine, yet not at all demure. She has a provocative pose with her legs open. It represents everything I talk about in Feeling Myself – releasing the shame of our bodies, of our sexuality and not hiding it away."

Tell me about a sculpture you own...
"It was a gift from a friend who owns a gallery. It's by Polly Verity and is a depiction of two people kissing, made from a single sheet of paper. I love the tenderness of it."

What's your one piece of advice on collecting art?
"Set a budget and stick to it. It's not difficult to do, as there are so many great pieces at affordable prices. Art doesn't have to be expensive to be good – I have pieces that cost just £50 on Etsy."

ART IS NOT JUST PAINTINGS

Not, long ago, a set of three ceramic flying ducks hung above a mantelpiece would have been condemned as terribly old-fashioned. But times have changed – today, many would consider those flying mallards to be a fun and quirky way to decorate a wall. They are not the only objects to have undergone a style transformation. Whether because interior design has embraced all things granny chic or because the popularity of the memory wall (see page 135) has made it stylish to hang a variety of objects, today it is not just typical artworks that can be found on the walls of stylish homes.

Now everything from plates to hats and tea towels/dish towels can be treated as wall art. Many of these items can be bought inexpensively at markets and vintage shops, making them a cost-effective way to decorate. If you think outside the box, there are so many things you can introduce into the mix to create a space that truly reflects you and your personality.

PLATE UP

Ceramics hung on a wall really have undergone a style transformation and none more so than plates. Although they are a natural fit for kitchen and dining areas, they can also be found decorating hallways, living rooms and bathrooms. Plates in a traditional pattern such as the well-known blue-and-white Willow motif or toile de Jouy suit a more classic or country look although they're also a good way to add a dash of old to a modern space. For a more contemporary look, there are now many chic designs available; in fact, some are so lovely that it seems a waste to stash them away in a cupboard!

When it comes to displaying plates, you can either mix designs in differing patterns and colours or choose plates in just one hue for a striking monochrome look. You can cover an entire wall or just a section in a loose, free-flowing style, though it helps if you broadly follow a geometric shape such as a square, circle, triangle or diamond. If using plates in a range of sizes, place the larger ones at the bottom to create a sense of balance. Another option is to hang them in a grid or in a vertical or horizontal line. To keep the look cohesive, use plates that are linked by colour or style of pattern.

PAGES 156–157 This gallery wall is rich in decorative detail. The beautiful frames of the mirrors and lino-cut illustrations create a sense of cohesion, allowing the objets trouvés (shells, a key and a feather) to feel that they belong.

OPPOSITE A large painted whale with its gentle face and curving shape fills a living room wall. The portrait adds a pop of colour.

ABOVE A pale pink ballgown against a fluorescent pink mount/mat in an antique gilt frame creates a statement piece of art and evokes memories of a special occasion.

It's possible to make a beautiful wall using only round plates, but a mix of shapes can look and feel dynamic. If using monochrome plates, aim for those with a textured pattern so the display looks interesting. You can now buy invisible plate hangers and hooks so all the hardware is hidden away out of sight.

HATS OFF

A display of hats adds a bohemian vibe to a space and works particularly well in hallways, living rooms and bedrooms. Straw hats are particularly good for giving a room a relaxed feel, but make sure you mix up the styles of hat for added visual interest. Just be careful if using dark-coloured fedoras, as they can make a space feel heavy; they generally look better mixed in with lighter hues.

Baskets are also brilliant for adding texture, and as they come in bright hues, they add a cheering pop of colour to a room. Baskets look best hung close together, even overlapping a little. As a rule, with both hats and baskets, choose an odd number to display, as this gives a more natural feel; even numbers look too symmetrical and formal.

SIGN LANGUAGE

Old signs can evoke a sense of place or provoke a happy memory as well as introducing a different element into the decor. Large signs such as bus rolls will create a statement on their own and can be hung as a focal point or a second visual hit in a room. Smaller signs are great for lifting nooks and alcoves or the space above a door. They also work well as part of a gallery wall.

TOUCHABLE TEXTILES

Throws and blankets with highly decorative designs are
not just handy for cosying up a bed or sofa. They're also
just the thing for adding warmth and texture to a wall
or smooth surface. In a living room, throws and blankets
work particularly well behind a sofa, or hung up in the
corner of the space to create a snug area for reading. In
a bedroom, a throw hanging behind a bed can double
up as an alternative to a headboard.

Choose a throw that fits with the palette of your room.
Hang it using a baton or hide the fitting altogether by
fixing a length of carpet edging to the wall and then
carefully attaching the throw to it. Even tea towels/dish
towels can be framed to make eye-catching art for a
kitchen. Just make sure you iron out all the creases first.

OPPOSITE LEFT Maps make
excellent wall art – the contours
and shading create an image
that is full of texture and
interest. You can find a map to
suit any style of interior. One in
soft colours is just the thing in
this rustic-style home.

OPPOSITE RIGHT Mirrors
are another brilliant way to
decorate a wall. Not only do
they add great shapes, as in
this unusual display, they also
help bounce the light around
the room for a brightening
effect and can even make a
space feel larger than it is.

ABOVE LEFT Vases in a variety
of forms work like sculptures,
adding a three-dimensional
element to the room. Here,
blue vases with similar slim
necks are teamed with curvy
glass vases and ceramics for
a soft contrast to the filing
cabinets below.

ABOVE RIGHT A wonderful
mix of objects comes together
in this inspiring office, where
the display moves seamlessly
from the desk to the wall. The
smaller items are anchored by
a few larger pieces, including
illustrations by Martin Bourne.

ISSINGTON ZOO

ACTON — BRUNEL ROAD

ACTON — VIA DUCANE ROAD

MERSMITH BDY

ERSMITH — BROOK GREEN HOTEL

OOK — BRIDGE ROAD

IGSTON VALE

MALDEN — POLICE STATION

AMPTON — EARL SPENCER

AMPTON — BESSBOROUGH ROAD

RTH BROADWAY

CTON — HORN LANE

ON VALE — BROMYARD AVENUE

T CROSS — SHOPPING CENTRE

LE — ANNESLEY AVENUE

TION

A vintage London Routemaster bus blind becomes a large graphic artwork that decorates an entire wall. It complements the decorative wooden chair hanging on the wall, as well as the stacked suitcases and other old pieces. The black-and-white typography adds a cooler touch to the room.

COOL CORK

The drive for sustainability has made cork a very modern material and the corkboard a popular way to decorate a wall. It's easy and inexpensive to do. Simply stick on cork tiles or use pin-board/bulletin-board cork roll to create a wall and then attach your images, whether they be magazine pages, postcards or drawings. Use your corkboard wall in an office as an inspiration or for spaces such as hallways, style it up by placing a bench in front of it with an assortment of cushions/pillows.

SCULPTURE

Sculpture is an art form that is growing in popularity beyond expensive collectors, and while there are sculptural artworks you can hang, stand-alone pieces bring art off the wall and into a space, introducing an engaging three-dimensional element.

Marble and bronze are the materials most associated with sculpture but other often-used materials include stone, metal, ceramic and wood. Today's sculptors are also experimenting with the possibilities offered by more unexpected materials such as concrete, plastics and composites. One example that has been growing in popularity is resin, an inexpensive semi-transparent material that can be left in its natural state or painted to resemble traditional mediums such as marble, stone or bronze. Another is Jesmonite, a composite material that, like resin, can be easily moulded and finished in a range of textures and colours.

RIGHT With its feathery appearance, the Cameroonian headdress called a Juju hat adds a highly textured wall decoration. In this room, it injects a fabulous shot of bright red, the colour also found in the artwork propped on the mantelpiece linking the objects on the sideboard/credenza to the rest of the decoration.

RIGHT A sculpture gives focus to this display on a vintage metal table. Its height bridges the gap between the smaller pieces and table lamp, as well as the space between the table and artwork, a still life in oils by Harry Holland.

OPPOSITE Framing children's footprints, made with brightly colour paint, has turned them into works of art that will always evoke memories. They fit perfectly between the two windows and with just a vintage armchair and side table in front of them, are the focal point of that part of the room.

ABOVE LEFT Pieces of exterior moulding decorate a section of this stairwell. Although neutral in colour, they bring eye-catching pattern and texture to the space. The one large piece below the window is balanced by the smaller ones on either side.

ABOVE RIGHT Shelves above a desk have become a series of fascinating still lifes thanks to the myriad of objects displayed on them. Framed pieces of vintage art are mixed with empty frames that are interesting in themselves along with glassware, ceramics and tin boxes. Anything can be decorative art if artfully styled.

Sculptures can be statement pieces that grab the eye as soon as you walk into a room or smaller ones that have a more subtle impact. Whatever their size, though, they should always be placed at eye level – on a pedestal if needed.

When choosing sculpture as a focal point, consider its scale – too big for the room and it will overwhelm the space; too small and it will lack impact. You also want it to stand out, so choose a piece that contrasts with the wall behind it and try to place it so that it can be seen from multiple angles.

Smaller sculptures look good on a mantelpiece or displayed on shelves. You can also place them on side tables along with a lamp that can light up the piece so you can appreciate it day and night.

RIGHT Plates don't have to be colourful to create a visually strong display. Here, although all the plates are in a creamy shade of white, they have a variety of shapes, patterns and sizes, resulting in a look that feels textured and subtly beautiful.

BELOW Why stash jewellery in a box when you can turn it into an art installation? Here, necklaces of various materials hung on a wall are a practical solution (no tangling!) and a lovely decorative element framed by artworks above and to the side.

OPPOSITE Vintage wooden trays and picture frames in a variety of tones and sizes create a highly textured and original wall display that also serves as shelving for small decorative objects. An added hook makes a spot to hang a dishcloth and neon signs add extra character.

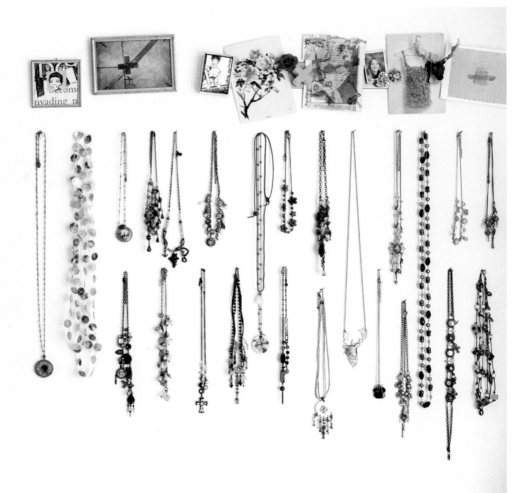

A large blanket easily and effectively decorates this high wall, adding a wash of colour and texture that warms up the space. The bright pinks, yellows and blues found in the blanket are reflected in the furniture around it, tying it to the room's decor.

LEFT Three colourful plates – objects always look better in odd-numbered configurations – pick up the colours of the kitchen, the plates perfectly suiting the function of the room and their fun motifs adding a playful touch.

BELOW LEFT A matching set of plaster reliefs gives this bedroom a three-dimensional decorative element. All in white and hung in a grid formation, they give a restrained rather than overly embellished look. The white is a sharp contrast to the deep blue of the walls but complements the crisp white of the bed linen. The vivid orange headboard offers an uplifting pop of brightness.

BELOW The straight lines and blocks of colour in the framed Union flag present a visual contrast to the squiggly red wallpaper in this bedroom. The flag also picks up on the graphic nature of the all-black door and grey skirting/baseboard. These elements create a room that is full of character.

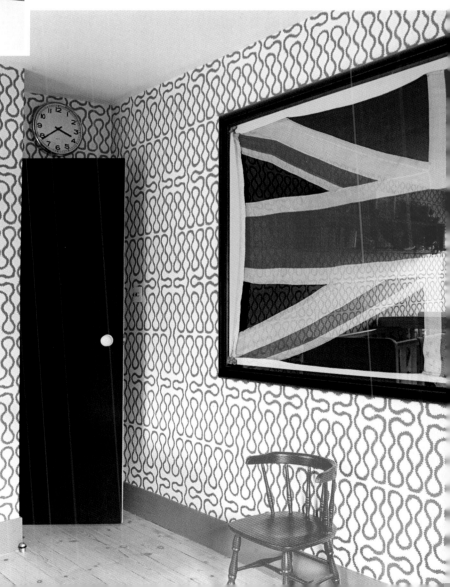

SOURCES

ONLINE

1000 Museums
1000museums.com
Museum-approved, archival-quality print reproductions of art from museums around the world.

20 x 200
20x200.com
Exclusively created limited-edition artworks by contemporary artists.

ArtFinder
artfinder.com
Over 10,000 works of art including paintings, drawings, prints, collages and sculpture.

Artfully Walls
artfullywalls.com
A large but curated collection of prints and original art including a wide range of pre-assembled gallery walls in a variety of themes. These can be customised by size and frame. Buy the gallery walls in their entirety or only specific works. Use the Wall Designer feature to create your own gallery wall.

Art Kiosk
glassette.com/collections/art-kiosk
Original art and prints with many works made exclusively for the online platform.

Art Republic
artrepublic.com
Limited-edition prints from a selection of artists, from emerging to established.

ArtStar
artstar.com
ArtStar works with a variety of contemporary creatives, including photographers, painters and mixed-media artists, to create a curated selection of limited-edition contemporary prints, available in four sizes. The styles on offer include abstract, fashion, architecture and landscapes.

Artsy
artsy.net
One of the world's largest online art marketplaces with almost two million works of art from emerging and established artists.

AucArt
aucart.com
Original artworks from emerging artists directly from their studios.

BetterShared
bettershared.co
Original art and limited edition prints from emerging artists from Africa and diaspora across the Caribbean, North and South America, and Europe.

Canopy Collections
canopy-collections.com
Original artworks by artists at all stages of their career.

Desenio
desenio.com
Prints and posters of Scandinavian design.

Etsy
etsy.com
Enormous range of originals, prints and posters as well as vintage art from paintings to maps.

Exhibition A
exhibitiona.com
Exclusive limited-edition prints from emerging and established artists.

King & McGaw
kingandmcgaw.com
Fine-art posters of works by major artists, both historical and contemporary, as well as photography and film, travel and exhibition posters.

Lumas
lumas.com
Limited-edition works from iconic photographers.

Murus Art
murus.art
A wide collection of limited-edition original prints and originals from both established and emerging artists. The art is curated into styles such as landscapes, graphic and botanical for easier choice. Use the virtual 'View on Wall' tool to see artworks in your space.

New Blood Art
newbloodart.com
Emerging artists in painting, drawing, sculpture and photography, including those newly graduated from art school, as well as mid-tier.

Partnership Editions
partnershipeditions.com
Prints and originals from emerging artists, with artworks exclusively handmade for the online platform and signed by the artist. Also pop-up exhibitions and workshops and advice on creating a collection.

The Poster Club
theposterclub.com
Inspired by Nordic lifestyle trends, a curated selection of prints and posters from emerging and established artists alike.

Print Club London
printclublondon.com
Handmade, limited-edition screen prints ranging from street art to graphic design and illustration.

PSTR Studio
pstrstudio.com
High quality posters and art exhibition prints across catergories including Japandi, Bauhaus, abstract and floral.

Rise Art
riseart.com
Paintings, drawings, installations, mixed media, photography, print and sculpture from emerging and mid-career artists.

Saatchi Art
saatchiart.com
Original works and prints by emerging artists. Prices range from the affordable to the upper end of the scale.

Society 6
society6.com
Wide range of reproductions of drawings, paintings, typography and photographs from independent artists.

Sonic Editions
soniceditions.com
Limited-edition prints of iconic photographs of scenes in fashion, film, music and sport.

SYNT
@seeyounextthursday
An auction house on Instagram. Once a week, art goes up for auction with the bidding happening in the comments.

Tappan
tappancollective.com
Original paintings, drawings and sculpture from emerging artists. Take the Art Style Quiz for personalized recommendations.

Uprise Art
upriseart.com
Original paintings, drawings, sculptures, commissioned pieces, and limited-edition prints.

GALLERIES

Eyestorm
eyestorm.com
Works from both established and emerging artists, including limited editions from big names.

Hauser & Wirth
hauserwirth.com
Limited-edition prints and archive exhibition posters.

The Met
metmuseum.org
The New York museum's custom prints shop sells reproductions of favourite and iconic images.

MoMA Design Store
moma.org
Posters and prints of iconic artworks, plus rare exhibition posters. An informative course on photography, too.

The Old Bank Vault
theoldbankvault.com
Contemporary art gallery that hosts exhibitions, private views, workshops and events. Hand-picked artists range from established names to emerging talent, and who work in a variety of mediums from street-art photography to acrylics and charcoal drawings.

The Photographers' Gallery
thephotographersgallery.org.uk
Exhibitions and sales of work from new and established international photographers.

Saatchi Gallery
saatchigallery.com
Posters, limited edition prints and merchandise that accompany its exhibitions.

Tate
tate.org.uk
Posters and limited edition prints of works in the Tate's permanent collection and special exhibitions and vintage exhibition posters.

VINTAGE

BLK MKT Vintage
blkmktvintage.com
Vintage art prints and collectibles that celebrate black history and artistic expression.

Curatorio
curatorio.co.uk
Vintage paintings, drawings and decorative pieces, in particular mid-century Scandinavian art.

The Discerning Palette
discerningpalette.com
Vintage modernist and modernist style art in a variety of categories including landscapes, nudes and still lives.

Etalage
etalage.co.uk
Oil paintings and rare prints as well as vintage posters and decorative objects.

Fabulous Vintage Finds
fabulousvintagefinds.co.uk
Paintings, both framed and unframed, along with second-hand frames, characterful signs, all sourced in France.

Fine Art America
fineartamerica.com
Enormous range of vintage art from canvas prints to framed, metal and acrylic, plus posters.

Medium Room
mediumroom.co.uk
Vintage paintings, drawings, lithographs and prints, and a wide selection of portraits.

Oil Archive
@oil_archive
Original oil paintings sold via Instagram, specializing in landscapes, still lifes and portraits.

Tarn London
tarnlondon.com
Range of framed vintage artworks, mostly in oils but with some drawings, too.

Vintage Art Gallery
thevintageartgallery.com
One off vintage artworks ranging from still lives to portraits and landscapes sold, in vintage frames, without being altered or restored. Paintings are shown styled for ideas on how the work in the home.

Vinterior
vinterior.co
Online marketplace of vintage and antique sellers from around the world, some of whom sell paintings, posters, photography, tapestries and sculpture.

FAIRS

Affordable Art Fair
affordableartfair.com
Art for all budgets with access to curators and artists. Three fairs are held in London, as well as in cities throughout Europe. Buyers further afield can attend fairs in New York, Singapore, Shanghai and Sydney.

Frieze
frieze.com
Four international art fairs each year – Frieze London, Frieze Los Angeles, Frieze New York, Frieze Seoul, all which focus on contemporary art while Frieze Masters (in London) showcases work before the year 2000. There is also Frieze Sculpture.

The Other Art Fair
theotherartfair.com
Held in London, Sydney, Melbourne and four American cities including Los Angeles, an artist-led fair that showcases works by more than 150 emerging artists across a range of disciplines.

Paris Photo
parisphoto.com
The largest international fair dedicated to photography with international exhibitors including leading galleries as well as established and emerging photographers. There is also Paris Photo New York.

Photo London
photolondon.org
The UK's biggest photography fair showcasing vintage and historic imagery from the world's leading photography dealers and galleries along with new talents.

Superfine Art Fair
superfine.world
A US-based fair held in cities across the country that is strong on inclusivity, with a significant representation of artists of colour, LGBTQ+ and female artists. The vibe is relaxed and the prices very affordable.

ART CONSULTANCY

Louisa Warfield Art
louisawarfieldart.com
A highly experienced specialist in the contemporary art market, working on a one to one basis to source modern, contemporary and emerging art for homes and offices. Create a collection from new or existing artwork.

PICTURE CREDITS

All photography copyright © Ryland Peters & Small 2023 unless otherwise stated.
Key: Ph = Photographer

Front cover Ph Dan Duchars/The London home of Catherine Ashton of @bo_decor; spine Ph Rachel Whiting/The home of interior designer Sarah Brown in London, sarahbrowninteriors.com; back cover Ph Chris Tubbs/The family home of Sarah Corbett-Winder, available to hire through Lavish Locations; 1 Ph Benjamin Edwards/The home of Jon and Louise Bunning of Mora Lifestyle; 2 Ph Beth Evans/The home of art collector Sara Lysgaard; 3 Ph Polly Wreford/The home of designer Anne Geistdoerfer (and her family) of double g architects in Paris; 4 Ph Polly Wreford/A family home in London designed by Marion Lichtig; 5 Courtesy of Artfully Walls/Artists: Christine Chitnis; Virginia Chamlee; Jackie Clark Mancuso; 6 Ph Polly Wreford/The home in Copenhagen of designer Birgitte Olrik of Rabens Saloner; 7 Ph Debi Treloar/The family home of Julia Bird in Cornwall; 8 Ph Jan Baldwin/Chris Dyson Architects; 10–11 Ph Rachel Whiting/Interiors design by Beth Dadswell of imperfectinteriors.co.uk; 12 Ph Polly Wreford/The home in Copenhagen of designer Birgitte Olrik of Rabens Saloner; 14 left Ph Rachel Whiting/Saša Antić – interior stylist, set and props; 14 right Ph Catherine Gratwicke/ Zoë Anderson, wagreen.co.uk; 15 left photo © Partnership Editions/Artist: Alessandra Chambers/Photography: Alicia Waite; 15 right Ph Polly Wreford/L'Atelier d'Archi – Isabelle Juy – l'atelierdarchi.fr; 16 above photo © Murus Art/Artist Frankie Thorp; 16 below Ph Benjamin Edwards/The house of Jon and Louise Bunning of Mora Lifestyle; 17 photo © Murus Art/Artists Jonathan Lawes; Marcus Aitken; Iona Stern; 18 Ph Rachel Whiting/The home of interior designer Jill Macnair in London, jillmacnair.com; 19 above Ph Debi Treloar/The family home of Ulla Koskinen and Sameli Rantenen in Finland; 19 below left Ph Polly Wreford/The home of the decorator Bunny Turner of www.turnerpocock.co.uk; 19 below right Ph Debi Treloar/The family home of Ulla Koskinen and Sameli Rantenen in Finland; 20 above Ph Polly Wreford/The home of interior designer Sarah Lavoine in Paris maisonsarahlavoine.com; 20 below Ph Katya de Grunwald/Sara Schmidt, owner and creative director of Brandts Indoor; 21 Ph Beth Evans/The home of Anders Krakau interior designer at Rue Verte, Copenhagen rueverte.dk; 22 Ph Polly Wreford/A family home in Islington designed by Nicola Harding nicolaharding.com; 23 Ph Beth Evans/The home of art collector Sara Lysgaard; 24 above Ph Benjamin Edwards/The home in Arundel of John Taylor and Barbara Cunnell of Woodpigeon; 24 below Ph Debi Treloar/Home of Tim Rundle and Glynn Jones; 25 above Ph Benjamin Edwards/The home of the designer and embroiderer Caroline Zoob in Sussex carolinezoob.co.uk; 25 below Ph Polly Wreford/ London house by Sarah Delaney Design sarahdelaneydesign.co.uk; 26–35 Ph Chris Tubbs/The family home of the jewellery designer Sandra Barrio von Hurter sandralexander.com; 36–43 Ph Katya de Grunwald/The home of the designer Dorthe Kvist meltdesignstudio.com; 44–45 Ph Debi Treloar/The home and studio of the Dutch architects Ina and Matt www.ina-matt.com; 46 above left photo courtesy of ArtStar/Design by TOV Furniture; art by Carla Sutera Sardo; 46 above right photo courtesy of ArtStar/photography by Brain Wetzel; design by Jan Talbot Design; art by William Wegman; 46 below photo courtesy of ArtStar/ design by Bennett Leifer Interiors; artwork by Tom Fabia; 48 left Ph Jan Baldwin/Artist Sandra Whitmore's cottage; 48 right Ph Benjamin Edwards/'Nautilis' is the home in Cornwall of James and Lisa Bligh

www.uniquehomestays.com; 49 left Ph Helen Cathcart/Illustrator and artist Maartje van den Noort www.maartjevandennoort.nl; 49 right Ph Katya de Grunwald/Sara Schmidt, owner and creative director of Brandts Indoor; 50 Ph Jan Baldwin/The home of Lucy Bathurst of Nest Design nestdesign.co.uk; 51 above Ph Catherine Gratwicke/The Madrid home of the interior designer Patricia Bustos de la Torre, instagram.com/ patricia_bustos, www.patricia-bustos.com; 51 below Ph Katya de Grunwald/The home of the textile designer Kim Schipperheijn in the Netherlands; 52 above Ph Rachel Whiting/Interior design by Beth Dadswell of imperfectinteriors.co.uk; 52 below Ph Beth Evans/The home of Creative Director and TV host Isabelle McAllister in Stockholm www.isabelle.se; 53 Ph Polly Wreford/A family home in west London by Webb Architects and Cave Interiors caveinteriors.com; 54 Ph James Gardiner/The Brooklyn home of Helen Dealtry of wokinggirldesigns. com; 55 above left Ph Debi Treloar/The home of artist Claire Basler in France; 55 above right Ph Polly Wreford/The home of Malene Birger in Copenhagen; 55 below Ph Polly Wreford/The home of the interior designer Sarah Lavoine in Paris maisonsarahlavoine.com; 56 above left Ph Helen Cathcart/Artist and designer Sarah E. Owen, saraheowen. com; 56 above centre Ph Rachel Whiting/The home of interior designer Sarah Brown in London, sarahbrowninteriors.com; 56 above right Ph Debi Treloar/Alan Higgs Architects; 56 below Ph Beth Evans/The home of art collector Sara Lysgaard; 57 Ph Rachel Whiting/The family home of Bella and Hugo Middleton, norfolknaturalliving.com; 58 above left Ph Catherine Gratwicke/The Madrid home of the interior designer Patricia Bustos de la Torre Instagram.com/patricia_bustos, www.patricia-bustos. com; 58 below left Ph Polly Wreford/The south London home of designer Virginia Armstrong of roddy&ginger; 58–59 Ph Catherine Gratwicke/The Madrid home of the interior designer Patricia Bustos de la Torre Instagram.com/patricia_bustos, www.patricia-bustos.com; 60 Ph Debi Treloar/The Brooklyn home of Martin Bourne and Leilin Lopez. Martin is represented by Jed Root LA, inc www.jedroot.com; 61 above left Ph James Gardiner/Elaine Tian of Studio Joo studiojoo.com; 61 above right Ph Polly Wreford/The home in Denmark of Charlotte Gueniau of RICE; 61 below Ph Rachel Whiting/Joy Cho – designer and blogger of Oh Joy! Ohjoy.com; 62 above and below left Ph Rachel Whiting/The home of interior designer Sarah Brown in London, sarahbrowninteriors.com; 62 below right Ph Rachel Whiting/The home of garden designer and author Dorthe Kvist, meltdesignstudio.com; 63 Ph Polly Wreford/The home of Victoria and Stephen Fordham, designed by Sarah Delaney, in London sarahdelaneydesign.co.uk 64 Ph Rachel Whiting/Niki Brantmark of My Scandinavian Home, myscandinavianhome.com; 65 left Ph Benjamin Edwards/The home in Arundel of John Taylor and Barbara Cunnell of Woodpigeon; 65 right Ph James Gardiner/The family home of Danielle de Lange of online shop Le Souk soukshop.com and lifestyle blog The Style Files style-files. com; 66 above Ph Rachel Whiting/The home and garden of Wil and Bertus Aldershof-Koch, Smidse Voorstonden Bed & Breakfast; 66 below left Ph Jan Baldwin/Designer Helen Ellery's home in London; 66 below right Ph Polly Wreford/A family home in west London by Webb Architects and Cave Interiors caveinteriors.com; 67 Ph James Gardiner/ The Brooklyn home of Helen Dealtry of wokinggirldesigns.com; 68 above left Ph Polly Wreford/The home of the decorator Bunny Turner of www.turnerpocock.co.uk; 68 below right Ph Polly Wreford/Cathie Curran Architects; 69 Ph Rachel Whiting/Karine Köng, founder and Creative director of online concept store BODIE and FOU bodieandfou. com; 70 Ph Katya de Grunwald/The home of Maaike Goldbach in the Netherlands; 71 above left h Benjamin Edwards/Home of Justine Hand, contributing editor at Remodelista, on Cape Cod; 71 above right Ph

Jan Baldwin/Designer Helen Ellery's home in London; **71 below** Ph Helen Cathcart/Artist and designer Sarah E. Owen, saraheowen.com; **72 left** Ph Debi Treloar/The home of artist Claire Basler in France; **72 right** Ph Helen Cathcart/The home of designer and author Anna Joyce in Portland, Oregon; **73** Ph Rachel Whiting/The home of artist/interiors consultant Russell Loughlan; **74 above left** Ph Helen Cathcart/The home and studio of jeweller Alix Blüh and photographer Michael Jang in San Francisco; **74 above centre** Ph Jan Baldwin/Ben Pentreath's London flat; **74 above right** Ph Rachel Whiting/Sophie Rowell, interior consultant @côtedefolk, cotedefolk.com; **74 below** Ph Jan Baldwin/Stylist Karen Harrison's house in East Sussex; **75** Ph Katya de Grunwald/The home of Emma Wilson in Sidi Kaouki, available to rent for photo shoots; **76 above left** Ph Polly Wreford/The family home of Elisabeth and Scott Wotherspoon, owners of Wickle in Lewes, www.wickle.co.uk; **76 above right** Ph Debi Treloar/The family home in Norfolk of Laura and Fred Ingrams, fredingrams.com; **76 below** Ph Polly Wreford/Cathie Curran Architects; **77** Ph Rachel Whiting/The family home of Camilla Ebdrup of LUCKYBOYSUNDAY; **78-87** Ph Dan Duchars/The London home of Catherine Ashton of @bo_decor; **88-95** Ph Polly Wreford/The home in Copenhagen of June and David Rosenkilde; **96-97** Ph Dan Duchars/The home of Samantha Thompson in London, @LondonStyleSisters; **98** Ph Beth Evans/The home of interior stylist Rikke Bye-Anderson in Oslo, rikkesroom.blogg.no; **99** Ph James Gardiner/Jeska and Dean Hearne, thefuturekept.com; **100 left** Ph Jan Baldwin/The Walled Garden at Cowdray, walledgardencowdray.com; **100 right** Ph Beth Evans/Kråkvik and D'Orazio, krakvikdorazio.no; **101 left** Ph Debi Treloar/The Norfolk family home of the designer Petra Boase; **101 right** Ph Polly Wreford/ The home of interior designer Sarah Lavoine in Paris maisonsarahlavoine. com; **102 above** Ph Rachel Whiting/The home of Desiree of VosgesParis. com in Rhenen; **102 below** Ph Rachel Whiting/Saša Antić – interior stylist, set and props; **103** photo courtesy of ArtStar/Interiors and art designed by Briggs Edward Solomon; **104** Ph Debi Treloar/Nikki Tibbles' London home. Owner of Wild at Heart – Flowers and interiors, wildatheart.com; **105 above left** Ph Debi Treloar/The home of Kristin Norris and Trevor Lunn, Philadelphia; **105 below left** Ph Beth Evans/Home of Daniel Heckscher, Interior Architect at Note Design Studio, Stockholm notedesignstudio.se; **105 below right** the home of Joanne Cleasby in Hove; **106 above** Ph Rachel Whiting/The family home of Bella and Hugo Middleton, norfolknaturalliving.com; **106 below** Ph Polly Wreford/ London home by Sarah Delaney Design, sarahdelaneydesign.com; **106-107** photo courtesy of Partnership Editions/Artists: Camilla Perkins, Venetia Berry, Emily Forgot, Mafalda Vasconcelos, Adriana Jaros, Rebecca Sammon/Photography: Alicia Waite; **108-109** Ph Chris Tubbs/ with thanks to For Art's Sake, forartssake.com/Artist Alex Arnaoudov; **110-121** Ph Chris Tubbs/The family home of Sarah Corbett-Winder, available to hire through Lavish Locations; **122-123** Ph Debi Treloar/ The family home in Norfolk of Laura and Fred Ingrams of fredingrams. com; **124** Ph Polly Wreford/The home of Ben Baglio and Richard Wilson in Suffolk www.benbaglio.com; **125** Ph Polly Wreford/The home of the decorator Bunny Turner of www.turnerpocock.co.uk; **126 left** Ph Polly Wreford/A family home in Islington designed by Nicola Harding nicolaharding.com; **126 right** Ph Rachel Whiting/Anne Hubert designer of La Cerise sur le Gâteau, www.lacerisesurlegateau.fr; **127 left** Ph James Gardiner/Maryanne Moodie; **127 right** Ph Polly Wreford/Interior design by Nicola Harding nicolaharding.com; **128** Ph Jan Baldwin/ Ben Pentreath's London flat; **129** Ph Beth Evans/The home of art collector Sara Lysgaard; **129 below** Ph Jan Baldwin/The London home of William Palin of Save Britain's Heritage; **130 above** Ph Jan Baldwin/ Ben Pentreath's house in Dorset; **130 below** Ph Winfred Heinze/The

apartment of Yancey and Mark Richardson in New York, Architect interior design by Steven Learner Studio; **131** Ph James Gardiner/Elaine Tian of Studio Joo, studiojoo.com; **132** Ph Rachel Whiting/Joy Cho – designer and blogger of Oh Joy! Ohjoy.com; **133** Ph Debi Treloar/Nikki Tibbles' London home. Owner of Wild at Heart – Flowers and interiors, wildatheart.com; **134** Ph Dan Duchars/The home of Samantha Thompson in London, @LondonStyleSisters; **135 above** Photo © Ashia Redhead of @no.2hastings; **135 below** Ph Katya de Grunwald/Sara Schmidt, owner and creative director of Brandts Indoor; **136 above** Ph Jan Baldwin/Stylist Karen Harrison's house in East Sussex; **136 below** Ph Chris Tubbs/The family home of the jewellery designer Sandra Barrio von Hurter sandralexander.com; **137** Ph Rachel Whiting/The home of artist/interiors consultant Russell Loughlan; **138** Ph Debi Treloar; **139** Ph Rachel Whiting/Designed by Armando Elias and Hugo D'Enjoy of Craft Design; **140** Ph James Gardiner/Jeska and Dean Hearne, thefuturekept. com; **141** Ph Polly Wreford/The home of the decorator Bunny Turner of www.turnerpocock.co.uk; **142 above** Ph Polly Wreford/A Suffolk home designed and styled by Sally Denning, sallydenning.com; **142 below** Ph Polly Wreford/The family home of Fiona and Alex Cox of www. coxandcox.co.uk; **143** Ph Rachel Whiting/The seaside home of designer Marta Nowicka, available to rent; **144 above left** courtesy of Artfully Walls/Artists Virginia Chamlee; Christy King; Martleen Kleiberg; Jackie Clark Mancuso; Ophelia Pang; **144 above right** courtesy of Artfully Walls/Artisits Michelle Adams; Ilana Greenberg; Georgesse Gomez; **144 below** courtesy of Artfully Walls/Artists Matthew Bowers; Christina Flowers; **145** Ph Rachel Whiting/Jonathan Lo, happymundane.com a nd j3productions.com; **146-155** Ph Chris Tubbs/ The home of content creator/author/speaker Natalie Lee of @stylemesunday; **156-157** Ph Debi Treloar/The home of jewellery designer and artist Ria Charisse dearswallow.com; **158** Ph James Gardiner/Jeska and Dean Hearne, thefuturekept.com; **159** Ph Polly Wreford/The home of Ashlyn Gibson, founder of children's concept store Olive Loves Alfie, interior stylist/ writer and children's fashion stylist; **160 left** Ph Benjamin Edwards/ Hannah Childs Interior Design, Old Lyme, CT, hannahchildsinteriordesign. com; **160 right** Ph Rachel Whiting/Designed by Stéphane Garotin and Pierre Emmanuel Martin of Maison Hand in Lyon, maison-hand.com; **161 left** Ph Rachel Whiting/The home of the stylist and writer Sara Emslie in London; **161 right** Ph Debi Treloar/The Brooklyn home of Martin Bourne and Leilin Lopez. Martin Bourne Stylist. Martin is represented by Jed Root LA, inc www.jedroot.com; **162** Ph Debi Treloar/The London home of Richard Moore; **163 above** Ph Polly Wreford/London house by Sarah Delaney Design, sarahdelaneydesign.co.uk; **163 below** Ph Polly Wreford/The family home of Sacha Paisley in Sussex, designed by Arior Design, ariordesign.co.uk; **164** Ph Polly Wreford/A family home in Islington designed by Nicola Harding nicolaharding.com; **165 left** Ph Jan Baldwin/Chris Dyson Architects, chrisdyson.co.uk; **165 right** Ph James Gardiner/Jeska and Dean Hearne, thefuturekept.com; **166 above** Ph Rachel Whiting/Sophie Rowell, interior consultant @côtedefolk, cotedefolk.com; **166 below** Ph Rachel Whiting/The home of Jane Schouten, owner of alltheluckintheworld.nl; **167** Ph Helen Cathcart/ Artist and designer Sarah E. Owen, saraheowen.com; **168** Ph Katya de Grunwald/The home of textile designer Kim Schipperheijn in the Netherlands; **169 above** Ph Catherine Gratwicke/The family home of Chris and Rachel Roberts in London, House designed by architects Office S & M; **169 below left** Ph Polly Wreford/A family home in Islington designed by Nicola Harding, nicolaharding.com; **169 below right** Ph Polly Wreford/The home of the decorator Bunny Turner of www.turnerpocock.co.uk; **176** Ph Rachel Whiting/Niki Brantmark of My Scandinavian Home, myscandinavianhome.com.

INDEX

Page numbers in *italic*
refer to the illustrations

ACKNOWLEDGMENTS

An enormous thank you to the art experts who patiently answered all my questions and corrected my misunderstandings – Erica Davis of Murus Art, Sim Takhar of The Old Bank Vault, Georgia Spray of Partnership Editions, Chrissie Crawford of ArtStar, Michelle Adams of Artfully Walls, Sara Allom of The Vintage Art Gallery, art consultant Louisa Warfield and Brian Davis of For Art's Sake. Thanks also to Chris Tubbs for his wonderful photography, as always. An equally huge thank you goes to the RPS team for allowing me to write this book, in particular Annabel Morgan and Leslie Harrington for saying yes, Sophie Devlin for her excellent editing, Toni Kay for the inspirational design, Jess Walton for her tireless picture research, Gordana Simakovic for ensuring production goes smoothly and the book hits the shelves (crucial!) and everyone who helped take *Art At Home* from idea to reality.